This Book Belongs:

- to a natural-born feeder
- on the kitchen counter
- to someone with impeccable taste
- in the Smithsonian
- to someone with the coolest friends

LET

ME

FEED

YOU

Everyday Recipes Offering the Comfort of Home

LET ME FEED YOU

ROSIE DAYKIN

appetite
by RANDOM HOUSE

Appetite by Random House® and colophon are registered trademarks of Penguin Random House LLC.

Library and Archives Canada Cataloguing in Publication is available upon request.
ISBN: 978-0-14-753108-7
eBook ISBN: 978-0-14-753109-4

Photography by Janis Nicolay
Photography on pages v, 24 (top left), 87, 104, 121, 155, 191, 216, 217, 231, 244 and 270 by Rosie Daykin
Illustration (place setting) on page 268 © LEOcrafts/Getty Images
Illustration (sandwich) on pages 94, 158, 162, 181, and 188 © ngupakarti/Shutterstock.com
Book design by Kelly Hill
Printed and bound in China

Published in Canada by Appetite by Random House®,
a division of Penguin Random House Canada Limited.

www.penguinrandomhouse.ca

10 9 8 7 6 5 4 3 2 1

appetite
by RANDOM HOUSE

Penguin
Random
House

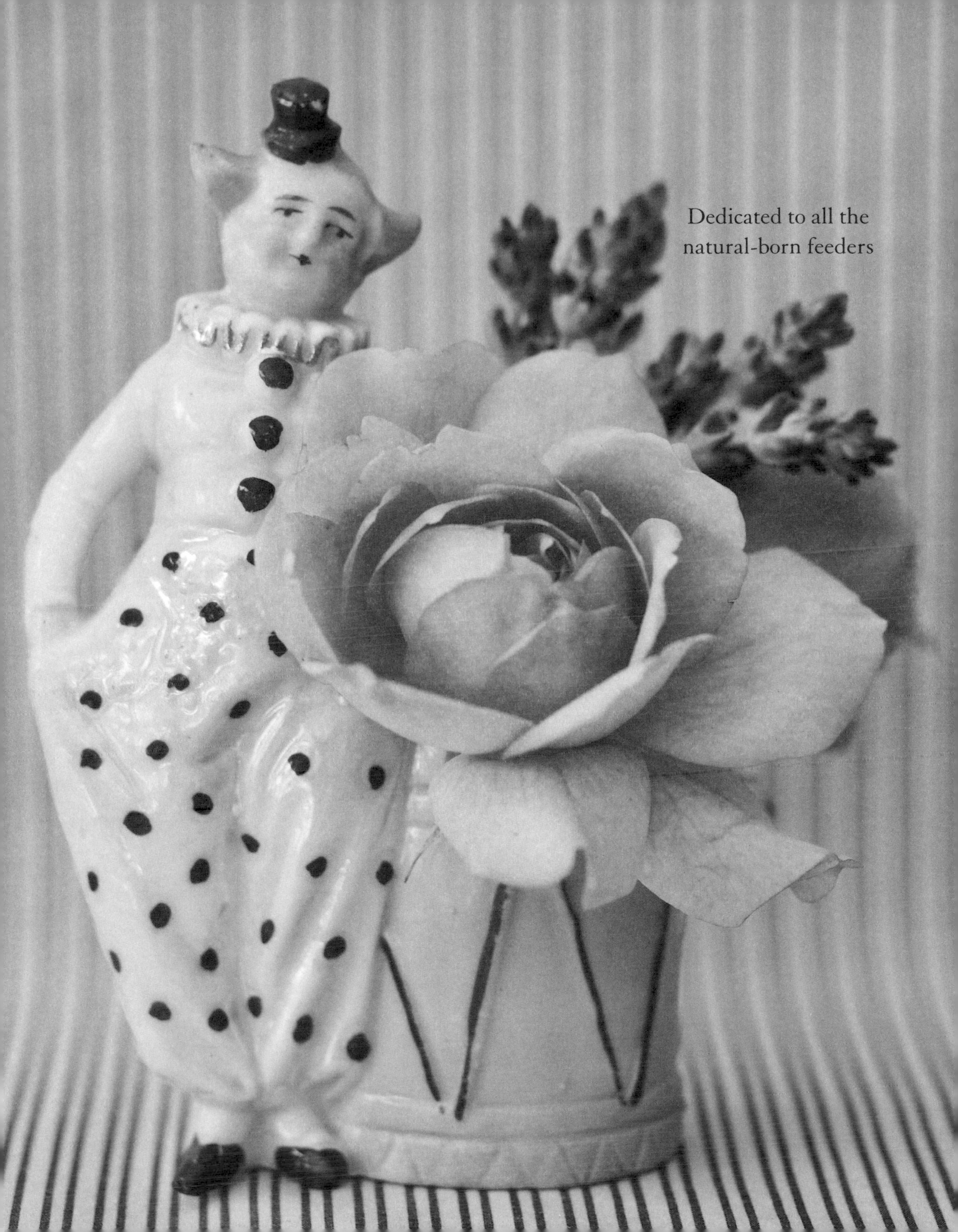

Dedicated to all the
natural-born feeders

TABLE OF CONTENTS

Let Me Feed You . . .

CHAPTER 1
Most Important Meal of the Day
BREAKFAST

CHAPTER 2
I'll Have a Chicken Salad Sandwich, Hold the Chicken Salad
BREAD, ETC.:

CHAPTER 3
There's No Such Thing as a Free Lunch
SANDWICHES

CHAPTER 4
Liquid Lunch
SOUPS

CHAPTER 5
Green with Envy
SALADS

Introduction

I am a firm believer that everyone is born with a certain skill. Born with it, not taught it. An education is a wonderful thing and we should never stop pushing ourselves to learn more, but some skills don't require textbooks and lessons, because we already possess them. From the moment we come screaming into the world, some of us will already understand music; some will have a knack for language; others will be naturals when it comes to painting or sewing or dancing or running. For some, the ability to make people laugh, or spell long and complicated words, will always be effortless. And for others—myself included—we will soon discover we are natural-born feeders.

I think my mum recognized this in me pretty early on. When I was 12, my parents took their first big holiday without their four kids in tow, and they were gone for two whole weeks. My older sister was left in charge of keeping an eye on us, but it was to me that my mum turned to hand all the grocery money over to. I'm sure the prospect of planning meals, grocery shopping, and feeding three siblings would have scared off most other 12-year-olds. But not me; I was thrilled. I still remember being down at the Food Barn, pushing what, in my memory, seems like the most enormous shopping cart up and down the aisles, grocery list tight in hand. I'm not going to lie; there weren't a huge number of vegetables consumed in my parents' absence, and maybe a few too many cookies and doughnuts, but I managed to keep us all alive for those two weeks.

As I grew, so did my love of feeding others. Ours was the house where all the neighborhood kids tended to congregate (no wonder my mum was exhausted). There was always an extra kid, or two or three, hanging about our house, which—given my penchant for after-school baking bonanzas—worked out pretty well. Those extra kids and I had what some might call a symbiotic relationship: their desire to eat cookies worked very nicely with my desire to bake them. And while baking was clearly my first love, I was always more than willing to whip up something a little less sweet if that's what the situation called for. I remember staying up late on countless Friday and Saturday nights as a young teenager, patiently waiting for my older brother and his buddies to return home so I could start churning out the grilled cheese sandwiches and hot buttered popcorn for them to eagerly consume. Suddenly the annoying little sister wasn't so annoying after all!

I moved into the first apartment of my own at the age of 19, and I'm pretty sure I was more excited about the prospect of throwing dinner parties than I was about my newfound independence. I loved that little apartment and its wee kitchen from the moment I laid eyes on it. Built sometime in the 1950s, it came equipped with a pink fridge and a little pink stove (which allowed you to control the heat of the elements via push buttons offering a wide range of options: low, medium, or high). It was from that very kitchen that I cooked for Paul and myself what, to this day, remains one of our most memorable meals. He swears he will never forget how delicious that roasted leg of lamb was, and I'll never forget how shocked I was that he damn near ate the whole thing! I'd like to think that the marriage proposal that soon followed was based entirely on Paul's undying love for me, but I suspect the lamb had more than a little to do with it (see page 188 for the recipe).

In 1989 Paul and I were married. Fortunately, Paul is a man who likes to entertain as much as I do, so as young newlyweds we hosted many a get-together for friends and family. The first home we shared was a rental—the main floor of a big old house not too far from the beach. Many of its original features were still intact, including a wood-burning fireplace, lots of dark wood paneling (which I boldly chose to paint white, and somehow the landlord never noticed), and a large dining room and kitchen. But for everything that was wonderful about the place, there were an equal number of oddities. For instance, the tiny little bathroom you accessed from the dining room was always bitterly cold, no matter the season; there was only one closet in the whole place; and I think the electric stove in the kitchen, given its dimensions, may actually have been meant for a doll's house. None of these quirks seemed to hold me back, though, and I willingly used all my spare time cooking and baking, trying out new recipes, and learning new techniques. This was years before the Food Network was on the scene, so I relied heavily on cookbooks, magazines, and a lot of trial and error to hone my skills.

As much as I loved mastering a new dish, I quickly recognized that my favorite style of cooking and baking was one with little fuss, using basic but quality ingredients. In 1993, when our daughter, India, was born, this approach became even more fitting as there was little time left in a day for anything more complicated. By keeping it simple and keeping it real, I managed to keep my sanity while still maintaining my love for feeding others.

Years later, I decided to go public with my passion, and in 2007 I opened my bakery, Butter Baked Goods. It was an adventure I had been dreaming about for much of my life, and I was thrilled at the prospect of finally being able to share the goodies I had been making for my family and friends with a wider audience. It would be a lie to say it was all easy going—trying to figure out how to feed so many people on a daily basis, given that I had no professional experience, took some practice!—but I'm nothing if not determined, and my hard work was rewarded by all of the happiness people found at the bakery.

I wrote my first book, *Butter Baked Goods*, in 2012, and my second, *Butter Celebrates!*, in 2014. Both books focus on the delicious baking we do day in and day out at Butter—the kind of nostalgic home baking that, if you're lucky, you'll remember from childhood. No mousse cakes or fancy pastries, just simple cookies, bars, cakes, and pies made using the best ingredients. Baking that reminds you that complicated doesn't necessarily taste better.

I'm sure that, for some of you who have gotten to know me through my previous books, it might be hard to imagine me outside of the bakery. Even those who know me personally are probably quicker to associate me with cake and pie than meatloaf and soup. I am, after all, the "Butter Lady." But bakers, like all humans, can't live on sweets alone. And my passion for baking really stems from my passion for all food, and for using food as a way to connect with others. I find that offering someone a meal, a snack, or simply a cookie is like starting an edible conversation when the chaos of everyday life prevents me from finding the words. Popcorn and grilled cheese sandwiches were a way for me to make small talk with the older boys when I was young, just as a big piece of lasagna and a glass of wine ask Paul to tell me about his difficult day now. Remembering to prepare India's favorite dinner every year for her birthday is just one of the million ways I tell her I love her, and so much tastier than words alone. Cooking for others has always been my way of communicating and demonstrating how I feel, and in a world chock-full of different skill sets, it's quite literally what I can bring to the table.

My hope is that you'll find the recipes in this book as delicious and satisfying as they are straightforward and achievable. I truly believe that even the most novice cook can find success with my recipes—for if cooking is a language, I try to avoid the big words. Given how busy everyday life can be, I don't believe that a comforting home-cooked meal should complicate it further. So I've got my fingers crossed that somewhere on these pages, you'll discover a favorite new dish (or two, or three . . .), and that you will be inspired to set the table, call for those you love to join you, and start a conversation of your own.

A Moment to Take Stock

I am not a huge fan of doing the giant, one-stop grocery shop. It's not so much the effort as it is the venue. I just don't enjoy spending a lot of time in big-box grocery stores. I appreciate that they often have the best prices on many staples, so I try to keep my pantry and refrigerator stocked with the following basics. Then I get my fruit, vegetables, and meat from smaller, independent stores every couple of days or so. This helps keep things fresh and means that I don't have to make up my mind so far in advance about what I'm going to cook that week.

When it comes to storage, I try as often as possible to transfer my dry goods from their original packaging into transparent airtight containers or canisters that are clearly labeled. Unsealed bags of flour and grains left in the pantry are invitations to moths to move in—a nightmare you truly want to avoid. Keeping things sealed also makes them last longer.

STAPLES

BAKING POWDER AND SODA Flaky biscuits and fluffy pancakes would be lost without them.

BREADCRUMBS I use regular breadcrumbs when making meatloaf, and like to use panko breadcrumbs for topping macaroni and cheese and breading chicken cutlets, for the crunchier finish they provide.

COUSCOUS, RICE, AND QUINOA All easy options to round out a weeknight dinner.

FLOUR It's always great to have a selection of flours (self-rising, whole wheat, pastry, etc.) on hand, but a bag of all-purpose will get you through most situations.

HERBS AND SPICES, DRIED A spice drawer or cupboard is one of those spots in the kitchen that can very easily get out of hand. Spices accumulate over time as we buy what we need for new recipes and then don't always work through them quickly enough. I encourage you to evaluate all your dried herbs and spices at least once a year, and toss anything you aren't using on a regular basis. The most commonly used herbs and spices in my kitchen are allspice, bay leaves, cardamom, chili flakes, chili powder, cinnamon, cream of tartar, cumin, curry powder, dried mustard, fennel seeds, ginger, Italian seasoning blend, nutmeg, smoked paprika, and turmeric.

HONEY Just as delicious on a piece of toast as it is in a dressing or marinade. I like to keep mine in the cupboard so it doesn't firm up and become too difficult to spread and scoop.

LEMONS It's hard to explain why, but my kitchen just doesn't make sense to me if I don't have a big bowl of lemons in it. As with salt and pepper, I am constantly reaching for them.

NUTS I try not to keep too large a quantity of nuts in the cupboard, as they will spoil, but I find it pretty easy to work through smaller amounts of cashews, almonds, pine nuts, and pistachios on a regular basis. Some end up in my cooking and baking . . . the rest end up in the palm of my hand.

OATS, STEEL-CUT AND LARGE-FLAKE ROLLED For breakfast or cookie making, or breakfast-cookie making.

OLIVE OIL I prefer extra virgin olive oil for my dressing, dipping, and drizzling needs, because of its superior taste and quality, but regular olive oil is just fine for frying or cooking. When you're cooking with it just remember it's best used for low and moderate heat only.

ONIONS, SHALLOTS, AND GARLIC Considering I am allergic to garlic and onions, it might seem strange that I insist on buying them, but frankly, some things are worth getting sick over (although I do try to avoid raw garlic as much as possible, which will help explain why my recipes don't often call for it). Most members of the allium family (with the exception of leeks, chives, and green onions) prefer to be stored in a cool, dry spot with ventilation instead of in the vegetable crisper in your refrigerator.

PASTA, DRIED For all that meat sauce you remembered to put in the freezer . . . right?

SALT AND BLACK PEPPER I keep my salt and pepper on a tray beside the stovetop so it is always within arm's reach. I have a small bowl of kosher salt for simple seasoning, baking, and salting pasta water, and grinders of sea salt and black pepper. I like to use sea salt when I'm preparing meat or roasting vegetables, and for sprinkling the top of focaccia bread, when I like the look and taste of its chunkier grind.

SUGARS It's going to be a lousy day if I don't have sugar in the cupboard! I always make sure to have both granulated and dark brown in generous supply.

TOMATOES AND TOMATO PASTE I always choose whole plum tomatoes over crushed; I figure the closer I can get to the original vegetable or fruit, the better, as it probably means the least amount of processing. I like to buy tomato paste in a tube instead of a can—some will suggest you get a more concentrated version in the tube, but honestly, for me it's just about the convenience of using what I need and then being able to put the cap back on.

VANILLA, PURE A necessary and heavenly flavor in 99.9 percent of all baking recipes.

VINEGARS I like a wide selection of vinegars to choose from, as each one can impart a slightly different flavor. Plain old white vinegar is fine when making pastry, but when it comes to dressings and sauces, I reach for wine, rice, or apple cider vinegar. I also love a good aged balsamic vinegar for some dressings or on its own, simply drizzled across the top of a dish to finish it.

WINE Mmmmm . . . yeah, yeah, I keep it in the cupboard just for cooking purposes.

YEAST I like to keep both active dry and instant (quick-rise) yeast packages in the cupboard so that bread and doughnut making can happen whenever the mood strikes.

CHILLY STORAGE

BACON If you have little else in your refrigerator, make sure there is bacon. Just a little goes a long way in improving the flavor of many dishes, whether you're making a quick pasta sauce, baking beans, or building a simple fried-egg sandwich.

CHEESE I'm not sure I could ever have enough cheese in my refrigerator, but if I had to choose three kinds that I use most often, they would be Parmesan, a sharp white Cheddar, and Boursin (I adore Boursin cheese in scrambled eggs or an omelet). Mind you, smoked Gruyère comes in pretty handy too, as does a tub of cream cheese. Okay, let's make it my top *five* kinds of cheese! Of course, if you're planning on making lasagna, don't forget about ricotta and mozzarella. Oh, damn . . .

CHICKEN STOCK If you have some chicken stock in the freezer, it's as good as having a pot of homemade soup on the stovetop. Stock takes a bit of work to initially make, but is such a huge time-saver after the fact. If you don't get around to making your own (see my Basic Chicken Stock recipe on page 99), just be sure to add some store-bought stocks to your pantry.

DAIRY My refrigerator is always well stocked with butter, whole milk, buttermilk, sour cream, and a smidge of heavy cream. Even if I am not planning a big baking day, I instinctively put butter in my cart at the grocery store, for I can't imagine a day going by when I won't need it. We always have a tub of plain, full-fat yogurt for Paul's breakfasts (I married one of those slim guys who gets to eat full-fat everything without gaining an ounce—totally maddening), but it also makes a delicious alternative to sour cream for topping chili or soup.

EGGS I like big brown organic eggs from free-roaming chickens. They might cost a little more, but I like to think that happy chickens lay tastier eggs.

FRUIT, FROZEN I always like to have frozen fruit available—it works just as well as fresh in pies and crisps, so be sure to tuck a little pastry in that freezer too.

HERBS, FRESH Dried are great and oh so handy, but nothing quite beats a handful of fresh herbs in pretty much any dish. I don't like to get caught without Italian flat-leaf parsley, basil, thyme, rosemary, mint, and dill.

MAYONNAISE It's pretty simple: Miracle Whip is not mayonnaise; Hellmann's is. (And no, this was not paid for by the makers of Hellmann's! I'm just a mega fan.)

MUSTARD Here's how it works: cheap yellow mustard for hamburgers and hotdogs (essential!); Dijon mustard for everything else.

PEAS, FROZEN I always like to have frozen peas on hand for an easy addition to soups, pasta sauce, and chicken pie (not to mention how handy a bag is to have for a burn or twisted ankle!).

Basic Bits to Get the Job Done

(plus a couple to make the job easier)

I had a good look around my kitchen, and while the following items aren't the *only* tools you're ever going to need to cook a meal, they will cover most of the bases. When I'm cooking, these are the tools I reach for time and time again. I don't really like to fill my cupboards and drawers with unnecessary gadgets and gizmos that only solve what are generally pretty simple tasks—I mean, that special little pincher thing that picks up pickles from the jar is really cool, but so is a fork.

BLENDER, IMMERSION BLENDER, OR VITAMIX Immersion blenders are great, and blenders even better, for blending soups and dressings, but nothing quite beats the power of a Vitamix. They don't come cheap, but once you've pureed your first batch of soup to silky smoothness, it gets a lot easier to rationalize the purchase.

CASSEROLE DISHES A good-quality oven-proof 9 × 13-inch casserole will cover a lot of your bases in the kitchen. Just make sure to buy one that you consider attractive for times when you serve family-style and are placing the dish on the table with your other serving pieces. I find that a simple white casserole dish works in most situations.

CAST-IRON SKILLET When Paul and I got married, a cast-iron skillet was his contribution to our kitchen supplies, and we are still using the same one more than 30 years later. Seasoned properly, a cast-iron skillet has an almost non-stick surface, and it easily goes from stovetop to oven and back. To season a cast-iron skillet, simply coat the pan with cooking oil and place it in a 350°F oven for about 1 hour. Remove it from the oven and wipe clean with paper towel. Avoid using dish soap and abrasive tools to clean it after each use, as these will strip away the seasoning.

COLANDER It should have holes. Ha! But seriously, given all the jobs that a good-sized metal colander will do in your kitchen, you really can't get by without one. From rinsing berries and grains to draining pasta and canned goods, or just washing salad leaves, you'll quickly appreciate its worth.

COOKIE SHEETS Being a baker, I can't say enough about buying good-quality, heavy cookie sheets. Higher quality means your pans won't warp in the oven and ensures even heat distribution. A couple of sheets will go a long way in the savory department, too, when you're roasting vegetables, cooking meatloaf, or broiling an open-faced sandwich.

CUTTING BOARDS I like to use plastic cutting boards for most of my chopping and cutting. They are lightweight, dishwasher-safe, and not too hard on your knives. I also like to give them a good soaking in diluted bleach water once a week to make sure to get rid of any bacteria and remove stains. Wooden ones are lovely, but generally much heavier and a little harder to sanitize, so I reserve them just for cutting bread.

DUTCH OVEN An enameled Dutch oven is another of my favorite pieces of cookware. Like the cast-iron skillet, it works wonderfully for braising meat, making stew, and baking beans, and its enamel finish cleans like a dream!

FLIPPERS I believe the proper technical term for this tool is "turner," but when I ask Paul to pass me the flipper-over-thing, he understands me just fine. Regardless of what you call them, you'll need a selection to conquer various flipping jobs. Pancakes and eggs need a wider flipper; steaks and burgers flip best with a slotted, metal version; and whole fish need a flipper with a nice long head so you don't break any delicate meat on the turn.

FOOD PROCESSOR I used to think of this as an extravagance, but given how much I use it on a weekly basis, I now see it as a necessity. As long as it's accessible and you don't mind the extra bit of work to keep it clean, a food processor can save you an enormous amount of time. From shredding vegetables and grating cheese to making pastry and dressings, all can be done in the blink of an eye.

JUICER A manual juicer is great to have on hand for smaller jobs like making salad dressing or freshly squeezing the smaller amounts needed when baking. Anything more than that and it might be helpful to invest in an electric juicer; your arm will thank you.

KITCHEN SCALE A scale provides true accuracy portioning dough. To ensure your Brioche Loaf (page 55) dough balls are exactly the same size before placing them in the pan to bake, or when dividing If Friday Were a Cake (page 235) batter evenly between two pans, there is no better way to check for accuracy than a basic kitchen scale.

KITCHEN SHEARS If scissors had a more skookum cousin, it would be kitchen shears. They are the perfect thing for snipping herbs, breaking down poultry, cutting up pizza, or simply cutting open a bag of frozen fruit.

KNIVES (A GOOD SET) I get through most jobs in the kitchen with a 10-inch chef's knife, a paring knife, an 8-inch carving or boning knife, and a serrated bread knife. The best knives are made with a single piece of steel and feel well balanced in your hand. Whether you're working with an expensive knife or not, the most important thing is that it has a sharp edge. Dull knives are a struggle to work with and can lead to nasty accidents in the kitchen.

MEAT THERMOMETER This takes the guesswork out of cooking meat. There is nothing more disappointing when carving into a piece (especially given the price of quality meat) than to discover that it's been over- or undercooked! The meat thermometer, like your mother, is always brutally honest.

MICROPLANE GRATER Always good to have at the ready for the oh-so-necessary lemon zest that seems to show up in most of my recipes. Be careful, though; they are crazy sharp.

NONSTICK SKILLET I love a nonstick skillet for frying eggs because I don't like my eggs cooked in butter or oil, but I also really appreciate it for the even browning it gives pancakes and English muffins. Just make sure to protect your skillet's finish by lining it with some paper towel or a dish cloth if you're stacking it with other pans.

PARCHMENT PAPER Truly one of the most-used items in my kitchen. I can never have enough parchment paper. If the world was ending and people were scrambling for supplies, I would be the lady stockpiling parchment paper. I always line my cookie sheets with it when roasting vegetables so that cleanup is a nonevent.

POTATO RICER If you want fluffy, perfectly mashed potatoes, you'll need one of these. It's a very simple kitchen tool used to process potatoes (and other foods) by manually forcing them through a fine metal sieve. No lumps—guaranteed!

POTS AND PANS There are an awful lot of options out there for pots and pans, but it's worth getting a good set. First and foremost you want a nice heavy set made from a combination of stainless steel and aluminum, as this gives you even heat distribution. I am a big fan of All-Clad, but there are definitely other choices. Pots and pans tend to be more economical to buy as a set than as singletons, but they're still pricey. If you're buying your pots and pans one at a time, focus on the following to start: 8-inch skillet, 12-quart stockpot with lid (perfect for making soups and spaghetti sauce or for cooking pasta), and 2- and 4-quart saucepans with lids. A large 6-quart sauté

pan with a lid might seem indulgent, but I find it really useful when making things like my One-Pot Chicken Parm (page 171) or when frying chicken cutlets, and it's nice to have that ample cooking surface when you need it.

SALT AND PEPPER MILLS As I mention in my pantry list (page 7), salt and pepper are always within arm's reach when I'm cooking. Ready-ground salt and pepper are vastly more convenient when baking, cooking, or salting pasta water, but I much prefer the flavor and look that grinding my own provides for finishing a dish. A quality pair of mills can be a little expensive, but they'll last you a lifetime.

TONGS A couple of pairs of simple metal tongs will go a long way in your kitchen. Use them for turning meat or fish in a skillet, coating pasta with sauce, lifting corn on the cob out of a pot, or dressing and serving a salad.

WOODEN SPOONS Can anyone ever have enough wooden spoons? (Paul, if you're reading this, don't answer that.) I love to cook with wooden spoons in all sizes and shapes, but they can be a little hard to keep clean. I put them in the dishwasher, which works just fine, but means over time they will crack and need replacing. (But hey, that just means you get to buy more wooden spoons! Yay!)

TELLING STORIES

I have always been a passionate baker, but I've only been a professional one for the last 12 years. In 2007, brimming with equal parts courage and naiveté, I decided to open Butter, which meant switching careers from my other life-long love, interior design. For some, it might have seemed like a big leap—to go from piles of throw pillows to mountains of butter cream—but I saw the logic in it. I'd still be creating comfort and joy, just with flour and sugar instead of paint chips and fabric.

To me the two professions have great synergy. The pleasure and reassurance that feeding ourselves and loved ones can bring goes hand in hand with the solace and support that home can provide. And while I might derive as much happiness from a delicious meal as I do the plate it's served on, I like to think that it's about something more than the overall aesthetics. To me, it's about a million little moments throughout the day that, when compiled, add a substance and fullness to our lives. Whether it's a hand-stitched quilt from Grandma or an enormous vase lugged all the way home from a European vacation; our possessions speak of our history, our dreams, and our passions, creating a reflection of our true selves. They don't have to be costly to make a statement, just simple things that help create a home and offer comfort and warmth. I'm not a huge "knickknack for the sake of knickknacks" kind of person, and I don't believe you can or should furnish a home in a day. I think if you allow yourself time to gather things that really resonate with you, that have meaning and hold memories, then your home will start to tell an honest story of who you are as a family.

Should you ever come to visit, and I've done my job right, hopefully you'll leave with a full tummy and good sense of what I, Paul, India, Pickle the dog, and Brian the cat are all about. I'll warn you now, let Pickle sniff your legs first before you try to pet her (to make sure you leave with all your fingers), and Brian is very shy so will no doubt hide in the basement only to emerge after you've gone. But in case we don't get the chance to hang out, I wanted the design of this book to tell some of that story in hopes that every time you open the front cover, it will feel like me opening the front door.

MOST IMPORTANT MEAL OF THE DAY

BREAKFAST

I'll never understand the kind of person who skips breakfast. Why would anyone want to shortchange themselves on a delicious start to the day? We need fuel to fly, people, and a cup of coffee won't get you far! My husband lives by this creed. If Paul Daykin was going to get a tattoo, I'd imagine it would be one of those retro-looking hearts with a ribbon draped across it, inscribed simply with the word "Breakfast." He loves breakfast. A lot. He puts an enormous amount of thought into it every day, so much so that he actually plans it the night before. Some people fall asleep counting sheep, but Paul is counting stacks of pancakes and bowls of oatmeal. Judging by the smile he wakes with every morning, I think the rest of us could take a page out of his book.

I absolutely love steel-cut oats, but I do *not* love that they take a while to make. Mornings can be hectic, and unless you're willing to give up an extra 30 minutes of shut-eye, regular steel-cut oats might be hard to swing on a weekday. At least it is for me, so I put my problem-solving skills to work and came up with this oat loaf recipe instead: steel-cut oats by the slice. Just slice, heat quickly in the microwave when you're ready to eat, and enjoy! A whole new take on instant oatmeal.

The Great Oat Loaf

Makes 1 (8-inch) loaf

6 cups water

½ teaspoon salt

2 cups steel-cut oats

1 teaspoon ground cinnamon

Place the water and salt in a large pot and bring to a boil over high heat. Add the steel-cut oats and stir vigorously to combine. Bring back to a boil, then reduce the heat, cover, and simmer for 15 to 20 minutes, until the oats are cooked through (they should be nice and thick). Lift the lid every 5 minutes or so to give them a good stir. Add the ground cinnamon and stir again.

Remove from the heat and gently pour the oat mixture into an 8-inch loaf pan. The top of the loaf will be slightly domed, but you can use a spatula to smooth it over. Cover with plastic wrap and let set in the refrigerator for at least 2 hours or overnight.

Once set, turn the loaf out onto a plate or small platter. Cut off a nice thick slice, heat in the microwave for about 1 minute, and top with your favorite oatmeal fixings. I like a big scoop of Strawberry Rhubarb Compote (page 22) and a little brown sugar.

Store, covered, in the refrigerator for up to 1 week.

*M*aking granola is so easy, you could probably do it in your sleep. But please don't try, because accidents can always happen. Some people like their granola with a little milk and fruit, others prefer it sprinkled on top of yogurt, and some of us, well ummmm, we eat it by the handful like it's popcorn.

Butter's Granola

Makes about 6 cups

3 cups large-flake rolled oats

1 cup unsweetened large-flake coconut

½ cup sliced almonds

½ cup pumpkin seeds

½ cup chia seeds

½ cup dark brown sugar

½ cup almond butter

½ cup pure maple syrup

¼ cup vegetable oil

1 cup dried sour cherries

Preheat the oven to 350°F. Line a cookie sheet with parchment paper.

In a large bowl, combine all of the ingredients, except the dried cherries, and mix well. You can use a spatula for this, but I much prefer to use my hands—it's both quicker and more effective at working the almond butter evenly through the oats.

Transfer the mixture to the prepared cookie sheet and spread evenly in one layer. Bake for 20 to 30 minutes, until the granola is crispy and a lovely golden brown.

Remove from the oven and let cool slightly before breaking up any larger chunks into smaller pieces. Let cool completely, then mix in the dried cherries.

Store in an airtight container in the pantry for up to 3 weeks. But if you eat it like popcorn, it's only going to last for 2 days.

*J*ust like butter and milk, I consider this compote a staple in my house. It's so easy to make and even easier to use up. It's the perfect accompaniment to a slew of breakfast options, like my Great Oat Loaf (page 19), yogurt and granola (page 20), pancakes, or French toast. I also like to fill my Breakfast Nest Cookies (page 36) with it, fold a scoop into some whipped cream, or spoon it on top of a slice of pound cake. It's even great with just a big ol' scoop of vanilla ice cream for dessert. Then, just like that, it's time to make another batch.

Strawberry Rhubarb Compote

Makes 1½ cups

3 cups chopped frozen rhubarb

3 cups frozen strawberries

¼ cup granulated sugar

1 teaspoon lemon zest

Place the fruit and sugar in a pot over medium-high heat. Stir to combine, and keep stirring for a couple of minutes until the sugar starts to melt and the fruit is warming up. Reduce the heat to medium, add the lemon zest, cover, and cook down for 10 to 15 minutes. Check in every 5 minutes or so to give it a good stir and reduce the heat further if necessary to avoid burning the fruit.

Uncover and continue to cook down, stirring constantly until the fruit is very thick and mushy (like a very loose jam), about 5 minutes. Remove from the heat and let cool.

Store, covered, in the refrigerator for up to 1 week.

PSSST ... *I prefer to use frozen fruit as it's more economical and means you can make this recipe year-round. You can mix up the choice of fruit if this combo isn't your favorite: peach and raspberry or straight-up blueberry are both delicious options.*

*T*he greatest excuses for leftovers in the world are often the hardest to come by. But should you somehow manage not to gobble up all of your fresh croissants the day they are baked, and find yourself in the possession of some day-olds, I strongly suggest you revive them with this recipe. Like most of us, they get a little more interesting with age.

Apple Almond Double-Baked Croissants

Makes 6 croissants

3 cups peeled, cored, and chopped (½-inch pieces) apple (about 3 large apples, something tart like Granny Smith)

¼ cup dark brown sugar

½ teaspoon ground cinnamon

¼ teaspoon salt

1 tablespoon butter

½ teaspoon lemon zest

6 day-old Homemade Croissants (page 61) or store-bought

½ cup sliced almonds, skin on

Almond Syrup

¼ cup granulated sugar

¼ cup water

1 teaspoon almond flavoring

1 teaspoon pure vanilla

Almond Cream

¼ cup butter, room temperature

½ cup granulated sugar

1 egg

⅓ cup all-purpose flour

½ cup almond meal (ground almonds)

Preheat the oven to 350°F. Line a cookie sheet with parchment paper.

Place the apples, brown sugar, cinnamon, and salt in a medium pot over medium heat and stir to combine. Cook until the apples begin to soften and the liquid has boiled off, about 15 minutes. Remove from the heat and stir in the butter and lemon zest. Set aside.

Make the almond syrup: In a small saucepan over medium-high heat, combine all of the ingredients and bring to a boil. Boil for 1 minute, then remove from the heat and set aside to cool.

Make the almond cream: Combine the butter and sugar in the bowl of a stand mixer fitted with the paddle attachment. Beat on medium speed until light and fluffy. Add the egg and beat to combine. Scrape down the sides of the bowl and add the flour and almond meal. Beat again on medium speed until well combined.

Using a large serrated knife, cut each croissant in half horizontally. Using a pastry brush, coat the inside of both top and bottom halves with the almond syrup. Spread the inside of each bottom half with about 1 tablespoon almond cream, then top with a generous tablespoon of cooked apples. Place the top half of each croissant back on, spread with another tablespoon of almond cream, and sprinkle with sliced almonds.

Transfer the croissants to the prepared cookie sheet and bake for 12 to 15 minutes, until golden brown.

*B*ecause sometimes even scones like to party.

Party Scones
(the ultimate birthday breakfast treat)

Makes 12 scones

Dough

4 cups all-purpose flour

2 tablespoons baking powder

1 teaspoon salt

1 cup butter, chilled and cut in 1-inch cubes

1 cup buttermilk

2 eggs

¼ cup rainbow sprinkles, plus extra for sprinkling

Glaze

1 cup icing sugar

1 to 2 tablespoons whole milk

Drop of red food coloring

Preheat the oven to 400°F. Line a cookie sheet with parchment paper.

Make the dough: Combine the flour, baking powder, and salt in the bowl of a stand mixer fitted with the paddle attachment. Give a quick turn on low to combine. Add the butter cubes and beat until large crumbs form.

In a large bowl, whisk the buttermilk and eggs together by hand. Add this mixture to the dry ingredients and beat until nearly combined. Add the sprinkles and mix again.

Turn the dough out onto a lightly floured work surface and gently knead a few times until it comes together. Using a rolling pin, roll out the dough to about 1 inch thick. Using a 2½-inch circular cutter, cut out 12 circles from the dough. Place the circles, evenly spaced, on the prepared cookie sheet.

Bake for about 15 minutes, until lightly golden brown and a wooden skewer inserted in the center of a scone comes out clean. Remove from the oven and allow the scones to cool on a wire rack while you make the glaze (you may want to place a piece of parchment paper underneath to catch any drips).

Make the glaze: Place the icing sugar in a small bowl and whisk in enough of the milk to create a runny glaze. Add the food coloring and whisk again to combine.

Spoon a tablespoon of glaze atop each scone and allow it to drip down the sides. Top with a few more rainbow sprinkles and let the party begin!

Store tightly wrapped or in an airtight container for up to 3 days.

I don't eat pancakes that often, and it's not because I don't like them. On the contrary, I don't eat pancakes that often because I love them so damn much. This recipe makes about 16 pancakes (or what I like to think of as a single serving). I have fancied them up a little here— with the lemon, thyme, and blackberry syrup—but feel free to omit all of that for classic, fluffy pancakes you can smother in maple syrup. The Blackberry Syrup is also lovely drizzled on top of a bowl of vanilla ice cream or puddled next to a piece of pound cake. Heck, you might even want a little splash in a glass of bubbly! To make these, you need either a large nonstick skillet or an electric nonstick griddle (my choice for sure).

Lemon-Thyme Pancakes with Blackberry Syrup

Makes 16 pancakes

¼ cup butter

1¾ cups milk

3 tablespoons fresh lemon juice

Zest of 1 lemon

2 eggs

2 cups all-purpose flour

¼ cup granulated sugar

1 tablespoon baking powder

2 tablespoons thyme leaves

½ teaspoon salt

1 recipe Blackberry Syrup (see below), for serving

Melt the butter in a small saucepan over medium heat or in a small bowl in the microwave for about 30 seconds. Set aside to cool.

Combine the milk, lemon juice, and lemon zest in a medium bowl or large liquid measuring cup. Set aside until slightly thickened, about 10 minutes.

Separate the eggs (making sure you don't get any yolk in the whites) and set the yolks aside. Place the egg whites in the bowl of a stand mixer fitted with the whisk attachment and beat until stiff.

Place the flour, sugar, baking powder, thyme, and salt in a large bowl and stir to combine. Add the thickened milk mixture and the egg yolks and stir until just combined (don't worry if it's a little lumpy). Add the cooled melted butter and stir again to combine. Gently fold in the stiffened egg whites (again, don't worry about a few lumps). Allow the batter to rest for about 10 minutes to help relax any gluten that has developed; this will give you a tenderer pancake (and we certainly don't need any more callous and uncaring pancakes in this world).

Heat a nonstick skillet over medium-high heat or set an electric nonstick griddle to 375°F. Both are hot enough when a few drops of water

Follow me

sizzle and dance on the surface before disappearing. If your skillet or griddle are not nonstick, melt a little butter first so your pancakes don't stick (but make sure the butter doesn't burn).

Scoop ⅓ cup of the batter onto the heated skillet or griddle for each pancake, in batches of two or three at a time. Cook for 1 to 2 minutes, until bubbles begin to rise to the surface and the pancakes are nicely browned. Gently flip the pancakes and cook for another minute on the other side.

For tastiest results, serve the pancakes immediately, nice and hot. Smother with lots of Blackberry Syrup and top with a dab of butter.

Blackberry Syrup
Makes 1 cup

3 cups fresh or frozen
    blackberries (see note)

¼ cup granulated sugar

1 teaspoon lemon zest

Place the berries in a blender and blend on high for about 1 minute, until berries make a nice thick paste. Transfer to a fine-mesh sieve set over a small pot. Use the back of a spoon or a spatula to press the paste through the sieve. You want to extract the juice into the pot and leave all the seeds in the sieve. (If you don't have a sieve, use a piece of cheesecloth doubled over and large enough to drape over the edges of the pot. Place the paste in the center, gather all sides of the cheesecloth together, and twist to extract the juice into the pot below.)

Add the sugar to the pot and bring the mixture to a boil over medium-high heat. Reduce the heat a little and simmer for several minutes, until thickened slightly and a syrup has formed. Remove from the heat and let cool for several minutes before using.

Store, covered, in the refrigerator for up to 2 weeks.

PSSST . . . *If you use frozen berries for this recipe, make sure they thaw completely before placing them in the blender.*

*O*kay, you might consider this a rather decadent breakfast choice, but if I were to call it "Eggs, Milk, Bread, and Fruit Pudding," you probably wouldn't bat an eye. This is an easy and delicious breakfast to make for a crowd. Assemble it the night before and then just pop it in the oven in the morning while you're making coffee and setting the table.

Jammy Bread Pudding

Makes 6 to 8 servings

9 (1-inch-thick) slices bread (I like my Brioche Loaf, page 55, but you could also use challah)

½ cup strawberry jam

5 eggs

3 cups milk

1 cup heavy cream

½ cup granulated sugar

1 tablespoon pure vanilla

¼ cup butter

6 to 8 strawberries, hulled and quartered

1 tablespoon icing sugar (optional)

Preheat the oven to 375°F. Butter a 9 × 13-inch casserole dish.

Cut each slice of bread in half vertically. Spread one half of each with strawberry jam, then top with the other half to create jam sandwiches. Lay the sandwiches in the prepared dish, three across and three down. They will be slightly overlapping.

In a large bowl, whisk together the eggs, milk, cream, sugar, and vanilla to create a custard. Carefully pour the custard over the sandwiches, soaking them all. If some of the bread is poking up a little, press it down gently with your fingers to make sure it all gets saturated with the custard.

Melt the butter in a small saucepan over medium heat or in a small bowl in the microwave for about 30 seconds. Using a pastry brush, coat the tops of the bread with the melted butter. Sprinkle the strawberry pieces randomly across the top. (If prepping the night before, cover the dish with plastic wrap at this point and refrigerate.)

Bake for 25 to 30 minutes, until the top is golden brown and the custard has set.

Remove from the oven and allow the dish to rest for a few minutes to avoid burnt tongues—and then sprinkle with icing sugar (if using) and serve.

PSSST . . . *Photo on pages ii–iii*

o if you're being interrogated about your breakfast choices you can honestly say, "I swear officer, it was just a muffin."

Cinnamon Doughnut Muffins
(in case I can't convince you to try a bran one)

Makes 12 muffins

3¹/2 cups all-purpose flour

1²/3 cups granulated sugar

5 teaspoons baking powder

1 teaspoon salt

2 eggs, lightly beaten

1¹/2 cups buttermilk

²/3 cup vegetable oil

2 teaspoons pure vanilla

1 teaspoon ground cinnamon

¹/4 cup butter, plus 2 table-spoons for coating the pan

Preheat the oven to 350°F.

Melt 2 tablespoons of butter in a small saucepan over medium heat or in a small bowl in the microwave for about 30 seconds. Use a pastry brush to generously coat the cups of a 12-cup muffin pan.

Place the flour, ²/3 cup of the sugar, the baking powder, and salt in the bowl of a stand mixer fitted with the paddle attachment. Give a couple of turns on low to combine. Add the eggs, buttermilk, oil, and vanilla and beat on medium until just combined.

Use a large ice-cream scoop to divide the batter evenly between the prepared muffin cups. Bake for 15 to 20 minutes or until a wooden skewer inserted in the center of a muffin comes out clean.

Meanwhile, place the remaining sugar and the cinnamon in a medium bowl and stir to combine. Set aside.

Melt the remaining butter in a small saucepan over medium heat or in a small bowl in the microwave for about 30 seconds. Set aside to cool.

Remove the muffins from the oven and allow to cool for only a minute or so. Use a pastry brush to coat each muffin with melted butter and then roll each one in a little cinnamon sugar.

Store tightly wrapped in an airtight container for up to 3 days, or in the freezer for up to 3 months.

*S*ure, Party Scones (page 26) are great, but hey, so is doing your business. I like to make a batch of these and eat a few hot from the oven, then individually wrap the rest to be frozen for brekkies on the go. They are extra-good warmed up and slathered with some cold butter.

Blueberry Bran Muffins
(oh, stop it, they're delicious)

Makes 12 muffins

½ cup butter

1½ cups buttermilk

1 cup oat bran

2¼ cups all-purpose flour

½ cup granulated sugar

1 tablespoon baking powder

½ teaspoon salt

¼ cup fancy molasses

2 eggs, lightly beaten

1 teaspoon pure vanilla

1 cup fresh blueberries

Preheat the oven to 350°F. Line a 12-cup muffin pan with paper liners.

Melt the butter in a small saucepan over medium heat or in a small bowl in the microwave for about 30 seconds. Set aside to cool.

In a large bowl, combine the buttermilk, oat bran, flour, sugar, baking powder, salt, molasses, eggs, vanilla, and melted butter. Use a large spoon or spatula to stir until just combined, then gently fold in the blueberries. Let sit for about 15 minutes to give the oat bran time to absorb some moisture, soften a little, and expand.

Use a large ice-cream scoop to divide the batter evenly between the prepared muffin cups. Bake for 20 minutes or until a wooden skewer inserted in the center of a muffin comes out clean. Remove from the oven and allow the muffins to cool slightly in the pan before transferring to a wire rack to cool completely.

Store, covered, at room temperature for about 1 week or in the freezer for up to 3 months.

*E*ating cookies for breakfast is now legal. Actually, it was always legal, but this recipe allows you to indulge without being judged for your lousy choices. Well at least your breakfast choices, that is . . . As for your decision to cut your own bangs, I'm afraid you're on your own with that one.

Breakfast Nest Cookies

Makes 12 cookies

1 cup large-flake rolled oats

½ cup almond butter

½ cup butter

¾ cup dark brown sugar

1 large egg

½ cup mashed banana
(about 1 medium banana)

1 teaspoon pure vanilla

½ cup all-purpose flour

1 teaspoon baking powder

2 tablespoons flaxseeds

2 tablespoons chia seeds

2 teaspoons ground
cinnamon

½ teaspoon salt

¾ cup Strawberry Rhubarb
Compote (page 22) or
good raspberry jam

Preheat the oven to 350°F. Line a cookie sheet with parchment paper.

Place the oats in a blender and blend on high until finely ground. Set aside.

Place the almond butter and butter in the bowl of a stand mixer fitted with the paddle attachment and cream on high speed until well combined. Scrape down the sides of the bowl and add the brown sugar. Continue to beat on high until light and fluffy. Scrape down the sides of the bowl and add the egg, banana, and vanilla. Beat again to combine. Turn the mixer to low and add the ground oats, flour, baking powder, flaxseeds, chia seeds, cinnamon, and salt. Beat to combine.

Using an ice-cream scoop, scoop up 12 equal-sized balls of cookie dough and place them on the prepared cookie sheet about 1 inch apart. Lightly press each ball down with the palm of your hand. Use your fingers to create a wide well across the top of the cookie, leaving a small rim of dough around the edge of the well. Fill each cookie with 1 tablespoon compote or jam.

Bake in the center of the oven for 12 to 15 minutes, until the cookies are golden brown around the edges. Remove the cookies from the oven and allow them to cool slightly before transferring to a wire rack to cool completely.

Store in an airtight container for up to 1 week or well wrapped in the freezer for up to 3 months.

*T*hese homemade granola bars are packed full of good things to help fuel you with energy, put a little pep in your step, and get you on the go! They're also a good choice for a lunch box (or your glove box) in case you need a little lift come midday.

Go Bars

Makes 12 bars

Butter for pan

2 cups large-flake rolled oats

1 cup whole almonds, skin on

1 cup unsweetened large-flake coconut

½ cup wheat germ

¼ cup chia seeds

¾ cup honey

¼ cup dark brown sugar

2 tablespoons vegetable oil

1 teaspoon pure vanilla

½ cup finely diced dried apricots

½ cup dried cranberries

Preheat the oven to 300°F. Line a cookie sheet with parchment paper. Butter an 8-inch square baking pan and line with parchment paper.

Spread the oats, almonds, and coconut across the prepared cookie sheet. Bake for 10 to 12 minutes, until lightly browned. Remove from the oven and transfer to a large bowl. Add the wheat germ and chia seeds and set aside.

In a small saucepan over medium-high heat, bring the honey, brown sugar, oil, and vanilla to a boil. Boil for 1 minute, then pour over the oatmeal mixture. Add the apricots and cranberries and stir with a large spoon to combine. Transfer the mixture to the prepared baking pan and, using your hands, press it down evenly (it helps to dampen your hands with a little water to avoid the mixture sticking to you as you work).

Bake for 25 to 30 minutes, until the bars are a lovely golden brown.

Remove from the oven and allow to cool completely before lifting the bars (still on the parchment paper) out of the pan. Use a large sharp knife to cut the bars into 12 equal portions.

Store, wrapped, at room temperature for up to 3 weeks or frozen for up to 3 months.

You know the one, don't you? That egg sandwich thing with cheese and bacon. I can't remember where I first tasted it, but I'm pretty sure a weird clown with red hair was my waiter.

Egg McWhatchamacallit

Makes 1 sandwich

1 Real English Muffin
(page 53) or store-bought

Butter

1 tablespoon Smoky Tomato
Relish (page 226)

1 tablespoon mayonnaise
(maybe a little less if you
don't love it as much as
I do)

1 egg

1 slice Canadian back bacon
(optional)

Salt and pepper

Couple of slices sharp
Cheddar

Split and toast the English muffin. Lightly butter the inside of both halves. Spread the tomato relish on the inside of one half and the mayonnaise on the other. Set aside.

Generously coat the bottom edge of a metal cookie cutter (about 3½ inches round) with cooking spray. Place the cookie cutter in the middle of a nonstick skillet over medium-high heat. I always use a nonstick skillet, but if you use a regular one, lightly coat the pan with a little olive oil first. Crack the egg into the center of the cutter and use part of the shell to pierce the yolk and break it. Place the bacon beside it in the pan. Cook the egg until the white has set and the yolk is only slightly soft, about 2 minutes. Use tongs to lift and remove the cutter from the pan, then flip the egg. If the egg is cooked properly it should not stick to the pan. Give the bacon a flip when you flip the egg.

Remove from the heat and sprinkle the egg with salt and pepper. Top with the Cheddar and let sit for a few moments while the cheese melts. I find the residual heat of the pan finishes the egg nicely.

Place the fried egg and cheese on the lower half of the English muffin, then top with bacon. Sandwich it together with the other half and enjoy!

PSSST . . . *Using the cookie cutter isn't mandatory. If I'm in a hurry I don't bother, and just let the egg hang out of the sides of the sandwich. But if you're looking for something a little more uniform, the cutter is the way to go.*

Confessions of a
DISH ADDICT

On the long list of things to be addicted to, I bet you'd consider dishware to be a bit of a stretch. I mean, how far wrong can you go with pretty plates and bowls? As admissions go, this probably seems a tad dramatic, and you might be right. In fairness, I've never been strung out on bone china or found myself trying to hawk the stereo for one more Limoges platter. Not yet, anyway. On the surface, it might appear I am a woman of few vices. I don't smoke, I rarely drink, I've never been to the dog races, and being surrounded with sweets all day has dimmed my desire to consume them with abandon. I don't even know how to play poker. But lurking just beneath that "everything in moderation" demeanor lies a heart hell-bent on filling the cupboards to capacity with an excessive amount of fine china and vintage porcelain.

Like the proverbial moth to a flame, I am drawn in by every serving piece I see. The shelves sag as my stacks grow, much to my husband's dismay. "Rosie, we've got too many dishes." To which I say, "No, I don't think so, Paul. What we've got here is some poor craftsmanship and a serious lack of storage."

None of it is my fault, of course. I was raised this way. My mum felt that an education in dishes was just as important as the three Rs, so I spent more than a few Saturdays roaming the floor at Millar and Coe, an institution in Vancouver for fine china that is sadly long gone. My mum made a point of buying 12 different place settings, every one with a unique pattern, to expose her children to the variety and beauty that dishes can provide to every meal. It was an interesting study in personality to see which pattern each child naturally gravitated to and claimed as their own. My choice was Black Aves, a beautiful black and white allover pattern of birds and foliage that was equally graphic and feminine. Given my decisive nature, it only makes sense that I would choose to eat off the black and white ones.

Some lessons we learn really stick; some don't. I can't tell you much about dissecting a frog or quadratic equations, but I'll never forget how the right dish can enhance your meal—how much better your morning tea tastes in a beautiful cup and saucer, or how simple blueberries can be worthy of a still life portrait when served in a vintage bowl. Even as my collection swells, I never consider any of it too precious for everyday use. I'm one of those people who willingly throws the silverware in the dishwasher. I'm aware that this might shorten its life span, but at least I'll have had the pleasure of using it over mine. In the end, I like to think that my problem isn't so much an addiction as it is a philosophy. Surround yourself with things you truly love, use them, share them, and they will elevate your everyday moments for years to come.

I'LL HAVE A CHICKEN SALAD SANDWICH, HOLD THE CHICKEN SALAD

BREAD, ETC.

All good relationships require tending, and if you give them just a little time, attention, and love, I guarantee you will be justly rewarded. And so it goes with bread. I know that, to some, the idea of making bread seems a little daunting, but just like that fraudster the Great Oz, you'll soon discover it's just a nervous hotdog bun with a microphone standing behind that curtain. There will be highs and—if you leave your dough to sit in a cold draft or overheat the water for the yeast—there might be some lows. But hang in there! Be patient, and you'll soon know the peaceful, almost meditative state that comes when you're standing at the counter kneading warm dough. Or the satisfaction and relief that come when you watch it rise, inching slowly toward the bowl's edge, followed by an almost childlike joy as it deflates once given the necessary little punch to release all that air. The secret is just to follow the steps and treat your dough kindly, and before you know it you'll be spreading butter across a thick slice of hot bread with a smug look on your face.

*S*imple, basic, and delicious is the best way to describe this loaf. Don't get me wrong, I love a complicated, chewy bread chockablock full of hand-ground grains and a 30-year-old starter as much as the next guy. But sometimes I just want a couple of slices of fluffy white bread to build myself a meatloaf sandwich.

Good Ol' Fashioned White Bread

Makes 2 (8-inch) loaves

3 cups bread flour

2 packages (1½ tablespoons) active dry yeast

1 tablespoon butter, room temperature, plus more for bowl and pans

3 tablespoons granulated sugar

1½ teaspoons salt

2 cups warm water (about 120°F)

2½ cups all-purpose flour

1 egg

1 tablespoon cold water

PSSST... *When kneading the dough, fold the piece of dough in half toward you, then push it away from you again using the heel of your hands. Then turn the dough a quarter turn and repeat the process. You may need to sprinkle the counter with a little more flour as you go.*

Butter a large mixing bowl and two 8-inch loaf pans. Set aside.

Place the bread flour, yeast, 1 tablespoon butter, sugar, and salt in the bowl of a stand mixer fitted with the paddle attachment. Beat on low speed to combine. Add the warm water and continue to beat until well combined. Scrape down the sides of the bowl and beat on high for several minutes until the dough is forming but quite tacky and shaggy.

Change the paddle attachment to the dough hook and add the all-purpose flour. Beat on medium speed until the dough starts to come together. Turn the mixer to medium-high and continue to beat until the dough pulls away from the sides of the bowl and is smooth and slightly sticky, 5 to 7 minutes.

Turn the dough out onto a lightly floured work surface and knead it by hand until it's smooth and no longer sticky, about 5 minutes (see note). Shape the dough into a smooth ball and place it in the prepared mixing bowl. Turn the dough over once to coat it in the butter. Cover the bowl with plastic wrap or a clean tea towel and set it in a warm, draft-free spot on the counter. Let the dough rise until it has doubled in size, about 1 hour.

Punch the dough down to release the air inside. Turn it out onto a lightly floured work surface and let it rest for 10 minutes.

Divide the dough into two evenly sized pieces and, using a rolling pin, roll each piece into a rectangle, about 8 × 12 inches. Starting from the shorter side, tightly roll up each rectangle and place one in each of the prepared loaf pans. Cover lightly with plastic wrap or a clean tea towel and return to the warm, draft-free spot to rise until doubled in size again, about 45 minutes to 1 hour.

Preheat the oven to 375°F.

In a small bowl, whisk together the egg and cold water. Using a pastry brush, coat the top of each loaf with the egg wash.

Place the loaves on the center rack of the oven and bake until they're a lovely golden brown and make a hollow sound when you tap the top, about 30 minutes. Let cool in the pans for a few minutes before turning onto a wire rack to cool completely.

Store, tightly wrapped in plastic wrap, at room temperature for 5 to 7 days or in the freezer for up to 2 months.

*T*his is such an easy recipe with such rewarding results. It's perfect to serve as a simple appetizer with some olives and charcuterie, or alongside a big bowl of Italian Sausage Sauce Soup (page 119). I love this classic version just topped with salt and rosemary, but I wouldn't say no to adding roasted tomatoes and a sprinkling of goat cheese, or maybe even some caramelized onions.

Focaccia with a Salty Top

Makes 1 large (about 12 × 18-inch) focaccia

4½ cups bread flour

2 tablespoons granulated sugar

1½ teaspoons salt

1 package (about 2¼ teaspoons) instant yeast

2 cups warm water

¾ cup olive oil, plus more for bowl

Sea salt

2 tablespoons rosemary

Oil a large mixing bowl with olive oil and set aside.

Place flour, sugar, salt, and yeast in the bowl of a stand mixer fitted with the dough hook. Give it a couple of turns to combine. Add the warm water and ½ cup olive oil and mix on medium speed until the dough comes together. Increase the speed a little and continue to beat until the dough pulls away from the sides of the bowl and is smooth and elastic, about 5 minutes.

Shape the dough into a large ball and place in the prepared mixing bowl. Twist and turn the dough to coat it in the oil, then cover with plastic wrap or a clean tea towel. Place in a warm, draft-free spot to rise until it has doubled in size, about 1 hour.

Generously oil a cookie sheet with about 2 tablespoons olive oil.

Punch the dough down to release the air inside. Turn it out onto the prepared cookie sheet.

Cover with plastic wrap and let rest for several minutes to allow the gluten to relax, which will make the dough easier to shape.

Using the tips of your fingers, evenly push the dough to the edges of the pan. Cover with plastic wrap and let rise again until it has doubled in size, about 20 to 30 minutes.

Preheat the oven to 400°F.

Using a pastry brush, coat the top of the focaccia with the remaining olive oil (you should have about 2 tablespoons left). Use your fingertips to gently stipple the top of the dough to create random little wells, and sprinkle generously with the sea salt and fresh rosemary.

Bake on the center rack of the oven until lightly browned, about 20 minutes.

This bread is delicious hot from the oven but room temperature is just as fantastic. Should you be lucky enough to have leftovers, wrap in plastic wrap and store for up to 3 days.

*A*t Butter, we are famous for our marshmallows. I can't tell you how many people have asked me over the years, "You can make a marshmallow from scratch?" Which inevitably leads me to respond, "Of course. How did you think they were made?" I find English muffins are a little like marshmallows: a classic item we associate more with grocery-store shelves than we do our own kitchens. But, like the great marshmallow mystery, once you make your first batch of English muffins, you'll realize you now have one less item to add to your grocery list forevermore.

Real English Muffins

Makes 12 English muffins

Butter for mixing bowl and
 pan

3 cups bread flour

3 tablespoons granulated
 sugar

1 package (about
 2 1/4 teaspoons) instant
 yeast

1 teaspoon salt

1 cup water

1/4 cup whole milk

1 egg, lightly beaten

1 tablespoon olive oil

1/4 cup cornmeal

Lightly butter a large mixing bowl and set aside.

Place the flour, sugar, yeast, and salt in the bowl of a stand mixer fitted with the dough hook. Give it a couple of turns to combine.

In a small saucepan over medium heat, warm the water and milk to about 120°F; if it's too hot, it will kill the yeast (and you don't want that on your conscience).

Turn the mixer on low and add the warm liquid, beating to combine. Add the egg and olive oil and beat again. Scrape down the sides of the bowl. Turn the mixer to medium-high and continue to beat until the dough comes together and starts to pull away from the sides of the bowl, about 4 to 5 minutes. The dough should be quite soft and a little sticky.

Shape the dough into a ball and place in the prepared bowl. Give it a turn and flip it over so that the top of the dough is now lightly buttered. Cover with plastic wrap or a clean tea towel and let rise in a warm, draft-free spot on your counter until doubled in size, 1 to 2 hours.

Line a cookie sheet with parchment paper. Sprinkle the cornmeal over it and set aside.

Punch the dough down to release any air inside. Turn it out onto a lightly floured work surface. Divide into 12 equal pieces and shape

Over you go

each piece into a ball. Flatten each ball into a 3-inch disk and place in the cornmeal on the cookie sheet. Turn each muffin over once to coat both sides in the cornmeal. Cover with plastic wrap or a clean tea towel and let rise again in the warm, draft-free spot until they gain about 50 percent in size, 45 to 60 minutes.

Lightly grease a large cast-iron or nonstick skillet with butter or vegetable oil and heat over medium heat. Place several pieces of dough in the skillet and cook until they're a lovely golden brown, 4 to 6 minutes per side. Adjust the heat as necessary to avoid burning. Using a paper towel, wipe up any excess cornmeal left in the pan between batches to avoid burning it. (You can also use an electric griddle, which will fit six at a time, but I find the cast-iron or nonstick skillet creates much more even browning on the muffins.) Transfer the muffins to cooling racks lined with paper towel (to help absorb any excess butter or oil) and let cool completely (as hard as it might be to resist!).

Using a serrated knife or a fork, split the muffins open. Lightly toast in a toaster or toaster oven, smother with butter and jam, and enjoy!

Store, in an airtight container or wrapped in plastic, at room temperature for several days or up to 2 months in your freezer.

*J*ust like croissants, making your own brioche loaf is incredibly rewarding, and even more so if you arrange to have a crowd hanging around the oven door just as it's done! When you pull the brioche from the hot oven—with its lovely dark brown crust, all shiny and smelling of goodness—expect a lot of oohs and aaaahhs. Unless, of course, you're in France; they see this kinda stuff all the time.

Brioche Loaf

Makes 2 (8-inch) loaves

Dough

½ cup lukewarm water

2 packages (1½ tablespoons) active dry yeast

4½ cups all-purpose flour, plus more for bowl

¼ cup granulated sugar

1½ teaspoons salt

6 eggs, room temperature and lightly beaten

1½ cups butter, room temperature, plus more for pans

Egg Wash

1 egg, lightly beaten

2 tablespoons milk

Make the dough: In a small bowl, combine the lukewarm water and yeast and stir to dissolve. Set aside.

Sprinkle a large mixing bowl with flour.

Place the flour, sugar, salt, and eggs in the bowl of a stand mixer fitted with the dough hook and beat on medium to combine. Add the yeast and water mixture and continue to beat until the dough is smooth and shiny, about 15 minutes. The dough should be quite moist and will not form a ball. Turn the mixer to medium and add the butter, one tablespoon at a time. Beat until it is fully incorporated. The dough will be very sticky and shiny now.

Remove dough from the mixer and place in the prepared bowl. Cover with plastic wrap or a clean tea towel and set aside to rise in a warm, draft-free spot until it has doubled in size, about 2 hours.

Punch down the dough to remove any air inside. Cover tightly with plastic wrap. Allow to rest in the refrigerator for at least 2 hours or overnight.

Generously butter the bottom and sides of two 8-inch loaf pans. Set aside.

A lil' more work to be done

Remove the dough from the refrigerator and divide it into two equal halves. Divide one half into eight pieces, and gently roll each piece into a ball. Place the balls, side by side, into one of the loaf pans. Repeat with the second half of dough. Lightly cover with plastic wrap and let rest in a warm, draft-free spot until they have doubled in size, about 1½ to 2 hours.

Preheat the oven to 375°F.

Make the egg wash: Whisk together the egg and milk. Use a pastry brush to gently coat the top of each loaf.

Bake in the center rack of the oven until the loaves are a dark golden brown and sound hollow when the bottom of the pan is tapped, about 20 minutes. Remove from the oven (wait for the applause!) and let cool slightly before turning out onto a wire rack to cool completely.

Store, tightly wrapped in plastic wrap, for up to 3 days or in the freezer up to 3 months.

*C*orn bread is a delicious thing, even more so when you tuck a thick layer of cheese in the middle. I opt for Monterey Jack, but you can always switch it up with sharp Cheddar or any other firm cheese of your liking. Served warm from the oven, this makes the perfect side to ribs or a bowl of chili.

Cheesy Corn Bread

Makes 1 (8-inch) square loaf, 6 to 8 servings

1½ cups all-purpose flour

1 cup cornmeal

¼ cup granulated sugar

1 tablespoon baking powder

1 jalapeño pepper, seeded and finely diced

½ teaspoon salt

2 eggs, lightly beaten

1 cup milk

¼ cup sour cream

¼ cup butter, melted, plus more for pan

4 thick slices Monterey Jack (about 4-inch square each, or enough to make a single layer)

Preheat the oven to 425°F. Butter an 8-inch square baking pan and line with parchment paper.

In a large bowl, combine the flour, cornmeal, sugar, baking powder, jalapeño pepper, and salt. In another bowl, whisk together the eggs, milk, sour cream, and melted butter. Add the liquid ingredients to the dry ingredients and gently stir until just combined.

Spread half of the batter into the bottom of the prepared pan. Top with the cheese slices and then cover with the remaining batter. Use a small offset spatula or the back of a spoon to smooth the top of the batter so it's even.

Bake for 20 to 25 minutes or until a wooden skewer inserted in the center comes out clean.

Store, tightly wrapped in plastic wrap, at room temperature for up to 3 days or in the freezer for up to 2 months.

*O*h yes you can! I don't doubt for a minute that a lot of you will glance at this recipe and immediately think, "No way!" But, people, trust me. The only thing really challenging about making croissants is setting aside the time to do so. And even that isn't really a biggie when you consider the reward for your efforts: a pile of croissants, of course! So stick with me and I'll walk you through it.

Homemade Croissants
(trust me, you can do it!)

Sponge *(consider this the kick-starter for your croissants)*

1 tablespoon (1 and a bit packages) active dry yeast

1 cup water, room temperature

1½ cups all-purpose flour

Dough

3 cups bread flour

⅓ cup granulated sugar

2 teaspoons salt

2 small eggs, room temperature, lightly beaten

½ cup water, room temperature

2 tablespoons butter, room temperature

Butter Block
1⅓ cups butter, chilled

Egg Wash
1 egg, lightly beaten

1 tablespoon water

Makes 11 croissants (I know this seems like an odd number, but that's what you get)

Make the sponge: In a medium bowl, use a fork to combine the yeast, water, and flour. Cover with plastic wrap and set aside for 15 to 20 minutes.

Butter a large mixing bowl and set aside.

Make the dough: In the bowl of a stand mixer fitted with the paddle attachment, and with the mixer running on low, combine the ingredients for the dough (flour, sugar, salt, eggs, water, and butter) with the sponge. Increase speed to medium-high and continue to mix until the dough pulls away from the sides of the bowl and forms a nearly smooth ball, 5 to 7 minutes.

Transfer to the prepared bowl. Cover with plastic wrap and let rest in a warm, draft-free spot until it has doubled in size, about 1 hour.

This one's a real page turner

Turn the dough out onto a lightly floured work surface and, using a rolling pin, shape it into a 10 × 12-inch rectangle. Wrap the dough in plastic wrap, transfer it flat to a cookie sheet, and place in the freezer to rest for 20 to 30 minutes.

Make the butter block: Place the chilled butter between two sheets of parchment paper. Use your rolling pin to lightly pound the butter to make it pliable, then roll it into a 7 × 8-inch piece. Wrap the piece of butter in the parchment and set aside.

Remove the dough from the freezer. On a lightly floured work surface, roll the dough into a 10 × 18-inch rectangle.

Check the consistency of your rolled butter; it should be soft enough that you can leave an imprint when you gently push with your finger, but not so soft that you can push right through it. If it's too cold, it may break and tear the dough when rolling; if it's too soft, it will begin to ooze from the dough as it's being rolled. Neither of these situations will create the flaky croissant you're hoping for, so take your time to ensure that it's right.

Place the sheet of rolled butter on the lower half of the sheet of rolled dough. Fold the top half of the dough over the butter so that the butter is sandwiched between two layers of dough. Pinch all of the edges to seal it inside (this is known as the single-fold method).

Rotate the dough 90 degrees and, using a rolling pin, roll it out to a 10 × 24-inch rectangle.

Fold the top third of the dough down to the center, then fold the bottom third of the dough up and over top of that, as you would fold a letter. This is considered your first turn. Wrap the dough in plastic wrap and allow it to rest in the refrigerator for at least 1 hour. Resting the dough is very important as it gives the gluten that has developed a chance to relax and allows the yeast to develop and enhance its flavor.

Remove the dough from the refrigerator and repeat the whole process. Just as you did for your first turn, use your rolling pin to roll the dough out into a 10 × 24-inch rectangle and once again fold the piece

Nearly done

in three folds, as you would a letter. Wrap the dough in plastic wrap and place in the refrigerator for another hour. This is considered your second turn.

Remove the dough from the refrigerator and repeat the process one last time, thus creating your third and final turn. Wrap the dough in plastic wrap for the last time and let rest in the refrigerator for at least 1 hour or overnight.

Line two cookie sheets with parchment paper.

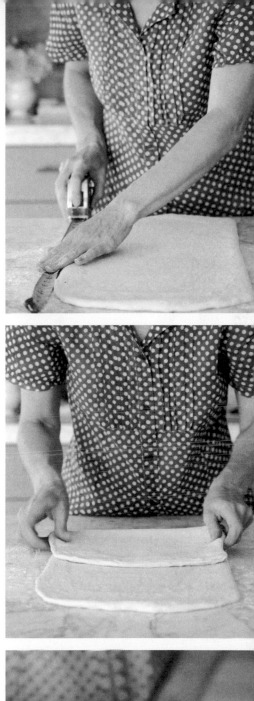

Remove the dough from the refrigerator, unwrap, and place on a lightly floured work surface. Roll it out into a 9 × 24-inch rectangle. Use a pizza cutter or a sharp knife to cut the dough into 11 triangles (about 9 inches long × 4 inches wide at the base). Use your hands to gently stretch each piece of dough to slightly elongate them.

Place one of the triangles of dough on your work surface and use your hands to gently stretch the widest end of the triangle a little, then begin to roll it up from the base to the tip. Place it on the prepared cookie sheet, seam side down. Repeat with each piece of dough. Divide the rolled croissants between the two cookie sheets so as not to over-crowd them.

Make the egg wash: In a small bowl, use a small whisk or fork to combine the egg and water. Use a pastry brush to gently coat each croissant all over with the wash. Place the remaining egg wash in the refrigerator until you need it again.

Leave the croissants to rise in a warm (but not too warm; we don't want to melt any of those lovely butter layers), draft-free spot until doubled in size, 1 to 1½ hours.

Preheat the oven to 350°F.

Use a pastry brush to gently coat each croissant all over again with the egg wash.

Bake for 15 to 20 minutes, until the croissants are a lovely deep brown. Enjoy hot from the oven with lots of butter and jam. See, wasn't it worth it?

Store the baked croissants, well wrapped, in the freezer for up to 1 month. Reheat them in a 300°F oven for about 10 minutes before serving.

I've often said that the only good excuse for acting flaky is if you're a biscuit. Short of that, I just can't tolerate that kind of behavior. This recipe calls for Cheddar, but it's not mandatory. With or without cheese, these are just as delicious alongside a bowl of Turkey Chili (page 161) as they are with a little fried chicken (page 162).

Fluffy Flaky Biscuits

Makes 12 biscuits

3 cups all-purpose flour

1½ tablespoons baking powder

1½ tablespoons granulated sugar

¾ teaspoon salt

¾ cup butter, chilled and cut in 1-inch cubes

1 cup grated sharp Cheddar (optional)

1½ cups buttermilk

1 egg, lightly beaten

Preheat the oven to 425°F. Line a cookie sheet with parchment paper.

In a large bowl, combine the flour, baking powder, sugar, and salt. Using a pastry cutter or two knives, cut in the chilled butter until the mixture resembles coarse crumbs and the butter pieces are pea-sized. Add the Cheddar if using and stir to combine. Add the buttermilk and use a fork to stir it in until the dough just comes together and is very shaggy.

Turn out onto a lightly floured work surface and gently knead a few times to incorporate any remaining flour. With your hands, press the dough flat until it measures about 1 inch thick. Use a 2½-inch circular cookie cutter to cut out 12 biscuits. You will need to reshape the dough once or twice to cut out all of them, so go gently and be careful not to overwork the dough. (Overworked dough will cause the chilled butter pieces to warm and melt. When the biscuits bake, the butter bits give off steam, which creates the layers and flakiness we're looking for. If you're concerned that your dough is getting too warm, place it back in the refrigerator for a bit to chill it up before continuing to roll.)

Place the dough circles on the prepared cookie sheet and use a pastry brush to coat the top of each one with the beaten egg.

Bake for 15 to 20 minutes, until the biscuits are firm to the touch and a lovely golden brown.

You can store these biscuits, tightly wrapped or in an airtight container, for up to 3 days, but I truly think they're best eaten warm from the oven.

hese delicate little cheesy crisps work just as well with a bowl of soup as they do with a glass of wine.

Cheddar Cheese Crackers

Makes 36 crackers

½ cup pecan pieces

6 tablespoons butter, room temperature

2 cups grated sharp Cheddar

¾ cup all-purpose flour

½ teaspoon salt

¼ teaspoon cayenne pepper

3 tablespoons black sesame seeds

Preheat the oven to 350°F. Line two cookie sheets with parchment paper.

Place the pecan pieces in a blender or food processor and blend on high until just ground. Set aside.

In the bowl of a stand mixer fitted with the paddle attachment, cream the butter and grated cheese on high until combined, 2 to 3 minutes. Scrape down the sides of the bowl. Turn the mixer to low and add the flour, salt, and cayenne. Continue to beat until combined, another 2 to 3 minutes. Add the ground pecans and beat again until everything has fully come together into a soft dough.

Use a small ice-cream scoop or a spoon to drop 36 equally sized portions of dough (about 1 tablespoon each) onto the prepared cookie sheets, about 1½ inches apart. Pick up each portion of dough and roll between your palms to create a small ball, then return to the cookie sheet. Use the underside of a glass (or two of your fingers) to flatten each ball into a disk. Top each cracker with a light sprinkle of sesame seeds.

Bake for 10 to 12 minutes, until the crackers are lightly browned around the edges. Remove from the oven and allow to cool slightly before inhaling them all. Sorry! I mean, let cool slightly before transferring them to wire racks to cool completely.

Store in an airtight container for up to 2 weeks or in the freezer for up to 3 months.

HOUSE RULES

1. Down-filled pillows and seat cushions are a must. One glance at their lack of structure and plump curves offers the promise of comfort before your backside has even made contact. And the lasting impressions left by those who sat before you serve as a little invitation to come sit down and rest a while.

2. Does anyone actually put coffee on the coffee table? I prefer weird and wonderful objects for people to interact with. I like things that make a person curious or cause them to laugh out loud. A book on monkey portraits I found at a museum always elicits a fun response, just as a half-finished puzzle begs you to complete it. And nothing is harder to resist than a small dish of tiny hand-carved wooden tops, patiently waiting for someone to take up their cause! I've yet to find anyone who can resist giving them a spin.

3. Pets on the furniture are my favorite accessory. There's nothing more peaceful to look at than Brian the cat curled up on our bed or little Pickle stretched out in a sunny spot on a sofa.

4. Clean windows provide a brighter outlook on life, regardless of the weather.

5. There is no easier or more effective way to transform a room than simply by adding flowers. The humblest of bouquets can elevate your mood and add a focus and light that would otherwise be missing from the room. Think of it not so much as treating yourself, but rather as treating your home, for if it had a voice it would thank you.

6. Most importantly, decorate your home to enhance your life, not to complicate it. Don't worry about the eventual wear and tear on your lovely belongings. Like laugh lines on our aging faces, it's just proof of a life well lived.

THERE'S NO SUCH THING AS A FREE LUNCH

SANDWICHES

When I first opened Butter, it was only a small storefront with a display counter, a cooler, and just enough room for a handful of customers. Five years later, I was lucky enough to find a location just a stone's throw from the original space, but large enough to fit some tables and chairs so I could finally invite my customers to sit and stay a while. Mind you, they didn't need much convincing once they tasted my meatloaf sandwich! Seats filled up fast as everyone discovered the wonderful salty crunch that potato chips offer when tucked inside a tuna sandwich, or how the buttery layers of a homemade croissant tame the subtle spice of curried chicken. You see a good sandwich, like a good person, is hard to resist, when it consists of different layers, whether crunchy, salty, bitter, or sweet.

RD

*I*s it weird that I'm telling you how to make a sandwich?

Roasted Veg Sandwich with Walnut Pesto and Goat Cheese

Makes 4 sandwiches

4 (4-inch) squares focaccia (page 50)

Butter (optional)

½ cup Walnut Pesto (page 227)

4 generous handfuls Roasted Veg (page 205), about ½ cup each

½ cup crumbled goat cheese

Cut each piece of focaccia in half horizontally and lightly butter each piece. Buttering the bread is optional, but it does prevent your sandwich from getting soggy.

Turn all the pieces over, butter side up, and generously spread half of them with walnut pesto. Top each pesto half with a handful of roasted vegetables. Crumble the goat cheese over the roasted vegetables and top with the remaining pieces of focaccia.

Use a large serrated knife to cut each sandwich in half, and enjoy!

PSSST . . . *If you aren't a fan of goat cheese, you could always substitute feta.*

y open-faced sandwich takes one trip to France and now insists on being called Tartine. I find myself muttering, "Oh please . . . I knew you when!" a lot these days.

Whipped Ricotta with Figs, Hazelnuts, and Honey

Makes 4 open-faced sandwiches

¼ cup hazelnuts

½ cup Whipped Ricotta (see below)

4 thick slices whole grain or sourdough bread, lightly toasted and buttered

8 fresh figs, quartered

¼ cup honey

¼ cup microgreens (optional)

Preheat the oven to 300°F. Spread the hazelnuts on a cookie sheet and bake for about 15 minutes, until lightly colored and fragrant. Remove from the oven and wrap in a clean tea towel to steam for about 5 minutes. Rub the nuts with the tea towel to remove most of the skins, but don't fret if some remain. Use a large knife to roughly chop the hazelnuts, and set aside.

Thickly spread the ricotta across the top of the prepared pieces of toast (there can never be too much for me!). Evenly spread the fig pieces across the ricotta and then drizzle them with honey. Now sprinkle with the hazelnuts and top with the microgreens (I encourage you to try them, because they add another texture to this already delicious sandwich and make for an even lovelier presentation).

Whipped Ricotta
Makes about 1½ cups

2 cups (15-ounce tub) full-fat ricotta

3 tablespoons olive oil

3 tablespoons fresh lemon juice

Zest of 1 lemon

½ teaspoon salt

½ teaspoon pepper

1 tablespoon thyme leaves

Place all the ingredients except the thyme leaves in a blender or food processor and blend on high until the ricotta is smooth and creamy, 3 to 4 minutes. Transfer the ricotta to a small bowl and fold in the thyme leaves.

Cover with plastic wrap and chill for at least 1 hour. (I usually can't wait that long, so I leave lots on the spatula to tide me over.)

Store, covered, in the refrigerator for up to 1 week.

You know that thing people say about being on your deathbed and not caring about how many hours you worked in your lifetime? It's true, I'm sure, but I am going to be curious about how many avocados I've consumed.

Butter's Avocado Toast

Makes 4 servings

4 thick slices whole grain or
  sourdough bread

Butter

4 medium avocados

1 teaspoon chili flakes

Zest of 1 lemon

Salt and pepper

4 radishes, thinly sliced

Toast the four slices of bread and lightly butter. I like to give my bread a good toasting so it has a little crunch in contrast to the mushy avocado.

Use a large knife to cut an avocado horizontally until it touches the pit. Use the pit as your guide as you cut all around the avocado. Pull the two halves apart by twisting in opposite directions. Use the same large knife to give the pit a little whack, then gently twist and lift it out (be careful here, people; I don't want anyone ending up in the emergency room). Use a spoon to scoop the avocado from the skin and place it in a small bowl. Repeat with the remaining avocados.

Use a fork to mash the avocados, but don't overdo it, as I think a few chunky bits are nice. Add the chili flakes, lemon zest, and salt and pepper to taste.

Spread onto the prepared pieces of toast, then top with the sliced radishes and another sprinkle of salt.

I like to tell myself that, one day, eating egg salad will be an Olympic event. That way I don't feel so bad when I'm inhaling it by the spoonful, because, you know, training is everything if you want to bring home the gold.

Classic Egg Salad Sandwich

Makes 4 sandwiches

6 large eggs

¼ cup mayonnaise

1 teaspoon Dijon mustard

½ stalk celery, finely chopped

1 teaspoon salt

½ teaspoon pepper

8 slices Good Ol' Fashioned White Bread (page 46), or 4 (4-inch) squares focaccia (page 50)

Pea shoots or finely shredded iceberg lettuce, for serving

Fill a medium saucepan half full with water and place it over high heat. When the water is at a full boil, use a spoon to gently lower the eggs into it one at a time. Allow the eggs to boil, uncovered, for 10 minutes.

Remove the eggs from the heat and carefully drain off the boiling water. Place the saucepan under the tap and allow cold water to run on the eggs for several minutes. Move the pan to the counter and let the eggs rest in the cool water for about 15 minutes.

Take an egg and lightly tap both ends on the edge of the sink, cracking the shell. Then gently roll the egg along the counter to crack the sides of the shell. Hold the egg under running cold water while you peel the shell off. Once all the shell has been removed, give the egg a little shake to remove any excess water and place it on a cutting board. Repeat with the remaining eggs.

Cut each egg in half and remove the yolk. Set the yolks aside. Finely chop the egg whites and place them in a medium bowl. Use your hands to crumble the egg yolks over the chopped whites.

Add the mayonnaise, mustard, chopped celery, salt, and pepper and stir to combine. Cover the bowl with plastic wrap and chill in the refrigerator for at least 1 hour prior to serving.

I love to serve egg salad on lightly buttered white or focaccia bread with a handful of pea shoots, or in a mound atop some finely shredded iceberg lettuce. (But if you really want a treat, try scooping some up with a potato chip . . . it's the way we athletes like to eat it best.)

Store the egg salad, covered, in the refrigerator for up to 3 days.

*B*utter's curried chicken has always proven to be one of the most popular lunch options at the bakery, especially when stuffed inside one of our flaky croissants. A big scoop atop an arugula salad also makes a delicious and slightly lighter alternative.

Curried Chicken Sandwich

Makes 4 sandwiches

1 bone-in, skin-on chicken breast

2 teaspoons salt

1 teaspoon pepper

1 tablespoon olive oil

1 large stalk celery, finely diced

¼ cup dried cranberries

¼ cup roughly chopped walnut pieces

1 small green apple with skin, finely chopped in ½-inch pieces

1 green onion, white and light green parts only, finely chopped

½ cup mayonnaise

2 to 3 teaspoons curry powder (depending on how strong you like it)

Zest of 1 lemon

4 Homemade Croissants (page 61) or store-bought

Butter

Microgreens (optional)

Preheat the oven to 400°F. Line a cookie sheet with parchment paper.

Place the chicken breast skin side up on the prepared cookie sheet. Sprinkle the breast with 1 teaspoon salt and ½ teaspoon pepper and drizzle with olive oil. Bake for 25 to 30 minutes, until starting to brown and firm to the touch. Remove from the oven and allow the chicken to rest until cool enough to handle.

Remove the skin and pull the chicken from the bone of each breast. Use a large knife to cut the chicken into small cubes, about ½ inch square. Place the cut-up chicken in a large bowl.

Add the diced celery, cranberries, walnuts, apples, green onions, mayo, curry powder, lemon zest, and remaining 1 teaspoon salt and ½ teaspoon pepper, and stir to combine. Cover and chill in the refrigerator for at least 1 hour prior to serving to allow the flavors to meld.

Store the prepared curried chicken, covered, in the refrigerator for up to 3 days.

To serve, simply cut open a croissant, lightly butter, and top with a generous scoop of chicken salad and sprinkle of microgreens.

*P*otato chips: not so much a side thing as an inside thing.

Tuna and Potato Chip Sandwich

Makes 4 sandwiches

8 slices Good Ol' Fashioned White Bread (page 46), lightly buttered

Butter

½ cup Spicy Remoulade (page 222)

2 cans solid white tuna, drained

2 stalks celery, finely diced

Zest of 1 lemon

½ cup mayonnaise

Salt and pepper

Classic salted potato chips (I like Lay's)

Lay the bread slices on a cutting board or work surface and spread each with a thin layer of butter and 1 tablespoon of remoulade.

Place the drained tuna, celery, lemon zest, and mayonnaise in a small bowl and stir to combine. Season with salt and pepper to taste.

Spread the tuna mixture on half of the prepared bread slices. Top each one with a generous handful of potato chips and then the remaining slices of bread. Use a large knife to cut the sandwiches in half. If you're wrapping these sandwiches to go for a lunch or picnic, make sure to pack the potato chips separately so they don't go soggy. The salty crunch is what makes this sandwich so damn good!

Store the prepared tuna, covered, in the refrigerator for up to 3 days.

*T*his is one of my favorite sandwiches. If you're looking for something on the lighter side, skip the bread and just serve the shrimp inside a scooped-out avocado half.

Shrimp and Avocado Sandwich

Makes 4 sandwiches

3 cups peeled fresh shrimp, rinsed and drained

½ cup Spicy Remoulade (page 222)

2 avocados, thinly sliced

8 slices Brioche Loaf (page 55), lightly toasted and buttered

Salt and pepper

4 handfuls alfalfa sprouts (optional)

Place the shrimp and remoulade in a small bowl and gently stir to combine.

Use a large knife to cut an avocado horizontally until it touches the pit. Use the pit as your guide as you cut around the avocado. Pull the two halves apart by twisting in opposite directions. Use the same large knife to give the pit a little whack, then gently twist and lift it out. Use a spoon to scoop out the avocado from the skin and place it on a cutting board. Repeat with the remaining avocado, then thinly slice each half.

Spread the avocado slices across half the slices of the brioche and sprinkle with a little salt and pepper to taste. Spoon the shrimp evenly across the avocado, top with a handful of alfalfa sprouts (if using), and sandwich with the remaining slices of brioche. Use a large serrated knife to cut the sandwiches in half.

This sandwich stems from a delicious appetizer I once ate at our friends Bruno and Dianne's house. It was a long time ago, but if memory serves me, I ate most of the platter. Dianne was kind enough to share the recipe, which I tweaked just a little for a lunch option. If you want to serve it as an appetizer, just use baguette slices instead of a larger loaf (and make double if you're inviting me).

Tomato, Olive, and Asiago Broil Sandwich

Makes 4 sandwiches

4 cloves garlic, peeled

¼ cup olive oil

6 to 8 Roma tomatoes, seeded and finely chopped

½ cup finely chopped black olives

1 cup finely chopped basil

1 cup finely grated Asiago

4 slices whole grain or sourdough bread, toasted and lightly buttered

Preheat the oven to 400°F. Line a cookie sheet with parchment paper and set aside.

Use a piece of foil to make a little bowl, place the garlic inside, and drizzle with the olive oil. Pinch the top of the foil together to create a little pouch. Bake for 20 to 30 minutes, until the garlic is very soft and starting to caramelize around the edges. Remove from the oven and set aside to cool.

Place the roasted garlic and olive oil in a medium bowl and mash with the back of a spoon to make a paste. Add the tomatoes, olives, basil, and Asiago and stir to combine.

Place the slices of bread on the prepared cookie sheet and divide the topping between the slices. Place under the broiler until they're starting to brown and the cheese is melted and bubbling.

SANDWICH HACKS

(When leftovers become bestovers)

FRIED CHICKEN 2.0

Makes 1 sandwich

Take two slices of Good Ol' Fashioned White Bread (page 46) and spread a little butter on one side of both slices (butter on sandwiches isn't just about flavor; it also helps prevent your sandwich from getting soggy if you're packing it to travel). Spread one half of the bread with a generous helping of Lemon Aioli (page 221) or mayo and top with some shredded iceberg lettuce. Place a few slices of pickle on the other half (I like bread and butter pickles for this job) and top with a piece of chicken cutlet (page 162) and some freshly sliced tomato. Bring it all together and enjoy!

I'D RATHER EAT A C.A.B. THAN AN UBER

Makes 1 sandwich

Roasted Chicken (page 164) is delicious, but you know what makes it even better? Bacon and avocado. Honestly, bacon and avocado make everything better. I like to use two slices of a chewy sourdough bread for this sandwich. Butter both slices, then top one with mayo (I'm a big Hellmann's fan) and the other with a little Dijon mustard. Should you happen to have some leftover Dijon Herb Butter (page 229), you could always use that instead of plain old butter and skip adding the extra mustard. Finish with slices of roasted chicken (page 164), a couple of thick pieces of cooked bacon, and half of a perfectly ripe avocado, sliced. Sprinkle with a little salt and pepper and add a cap of fresh butter lettuce.

SOMETHING FOR YOUR HONEYMOON LAMB

Makes 1 sandwich

The next time you have a dinner party and serve How to Catch a Husband Lamb (page 188), try to save a little for lunch the next day. The secret to this sandwich is the pesto sauce. Simply make my recipe for Walnut Pesto (page 227), but replace the basil with fresh mint. I like to use a chewier bread like ciabatta for this sandwich. Butter the bread and smother in minty pesto, thin slices of lamb, and a sprinkle of arugula.

PARADISE BY THE DASHBOARD LIGHT MEATLOAF

Makes 1 sandwich

One of the best parts of having meatloaf for dinner is thinking about lunch the next day. Meatloaf sandwiches are hugely popular in my house, and once you taste one, you'll understand why. Spread two pieces of Good Ol' Fashioned White Bread (page 46) with butter, mayo, and Smoky Tomato Relish (page 226), then top with a thick slice of meatloaf (page 181) and a generous handful of thinly sliced iceberg lettuce. If you happen to have some Roasted Cherry Tomatoes (page 196) left over, a spoonful of them in place of the relish is pretty damn fine too.

JUST FOR THE HALIBUT

Makes 1 sandwich

The next time you're buying halibut, consider picking up a smidge extra to try in this sandwich. Spread two pieces of Brioche Loaf (page 55) with butter and Tartar Sauce (page 223) and top with a leftover piece of Iron Skillet Halibut (page 158) and some shaved iceberg lettuce. If you have some leftover Roasted Veg (page 205), you can always add a scoop of those, or, as in my recipe for tuna sandwiches (page 88), consider adding a few potato chips for a little salty crunch.

LIQUID LUNCH

SOUPS

If I told you to go clean out your refrigerator right now, no doubt you'd give me the old stink eye and question what business it is of mine. A fair reaction, considering we probably haven't met. But what if I told you to go and make soup? Would you listen to me then? What if I asked real nice? What if I promised that there are few rules and that you can pretty much throw any old vegetables in the pot, cook them down, and then blend them up? Maybe just add some rice or pasta, a handful of chopped herbs, and a smidge of salt. Would you think that's a good idea? See, cleaning out the refrigerator isn't so bad.

I have created a recipe for chicken stock, but please know that when it comes to stock, pretty much anything in your vegetable crisper goes. Making stock is one of the most efficient ways to clean out the refrigerator. If it looks like it's beginning to wilt, into the pot it goes!

Basic Chicken Stock

Makes about 12 cups

2 bone-in, skin-on chicken breasts (about 1½ pounds)

1 medium onion, peeled and halved

4 medium carrots, halved

4 stalks celery, halved

2-inch piece fresh ginger, peeled

1 handful flat-leaf parsley

1 handful thyme

2 cloves garlic, peeled

1 tablespoon salt

2 teaspoons whole peppercorns

12 cups water

Place all of the ingredients in a large stockpot over high heat. Bring to a boil, then reduce the heat to barely a simmer and cover. Allow the stock to cook for at least 2 hours.

Remove from the heat and use tongs to carefully lift the chicken breasts out of the stock. Set aside until cool enough to handle. Once the chicken has cooled, carefully remove the bones and skin and cut or shred the chicken into small pieces. If you're not carrying on to make Noodle Chicken Soup (page 108), you can freeze the chicken until you want to use it, carefully sealed in a freezer bag, for up to 1 month.

Use a large slotted spoon or tongs to remove all of the cooked vegetables and seasoning from the stock. Place a fine-mesh sieve in a large mixing bowl or fold a large piece of cheesecloth several times and drape it across the top of the bowl. Pour the hot stock through the sieve or cheesecloth to remove the last bits of vegetables and seasoning.

The stock is now ready to make soup! It can also be stored in three (4-cup) sealed containers and frozen for up to 3 months.

Roasted Tomato Soup

Makes 6 servings

2 pounds Roma tomatoes, halved

¼ cup olive oil

1 tablespoon plus 2 teaspoons salt

2 teaspoons pepper

1 tablespoon granulated sugar

2 cups peeled and finely chopped onions (about 1 large)

2 cloves garlic, peeled and finely chopped

2 red peppers, seeded and chopped in ½-inch pieces

1 (28-ounce) can whole plum tomatoes

4 cups chicken stock (page 99 or store-bought)

1 tablespoon balsamic vinegar

2 tablespoons butter

½ cup finely chopped basil leaves

Preheat the oven to 325°F. Line a cookie sheet with parchment paper.

Lay the tomatoes cut side up on the prepared cookie sheet. Drizzle with 2 tablespoons olive oil and sprinkle with 1 tablespoon salt, 1 teaspoon pepper, and 1 teaspoon sugar. Roast for 60 to 90 minutes, until the tomatoes are starting to wrinkle and brown. Remove from the oven and set aside.

Place the remaining 2 tablespoons olive oil in a large pot over medium-high heat, add the onions and garlic and cook until soft and translucent, about 10 minutes. Adjust the heat to avoid the garlic or onion browning. Add the red peppers and continue to cook for another 15 minutes or so, until they begin to soften.

Add the roasted tomatoes, canned tomatoes, and chicken stock and bring it all to a boil. Reduce heat and simmer, covered, for about 15 minutes.

Remove from the heat and transfer the soup in two or three batches to your blender to puree. (You'll need a secondary mixing bowl or bucket to hold the pureed soup while you finish the other batches. If using an immersion blender, you can puree the soup right in the pot, but you won't get as smooth a finish.)

Return the soup to the pot over medium heat and stir in the remaining salt, pepper, and sugar. Add the balsamic vinegar, butter, and chopped basil and stir again. Have a taste and season with a little more salt if necessary.

Store, covered, in the refrigerator for several days or up to 3 months in the freezer.

*O*kay . . . I admit it. I jumped on the green juice bandwagon. It's my understanding that if I consume enough of it then one day I'll look like Gwyneth Paltrow. In an effort to speed up the process I created this soup so I could double down on my daily consumption. No signs of the transformation quite yet, but the soup is delicious.

Green Soup

Makes about 6 servings

3 tablespoons olive oil

2 leeks (white parts only), washed and finely chopped

2 tablespoons peeled and grated fresh ginger

1 bunch kale (about 12 stalks), center ribs and stems removed, leaves coarsely chopped

3 cups lightly packed baby spinach

6 cups vegetable stock

2 tablespoons miso paste

2 tablespoons almond butter

Finely grated zest of 1 lemon

Salt and pepper

Plain yogurt, for garnish

¼ cup finely chopped mint, for garnish

Heat the oil in a large pot over medium heat. Add the leeks and ginger and cook, stirring often, until the leeks have softened. Add the kale and spinach and cook, stirring occasionally, until the kale is very tender, 12 to 15 minutes. Add the vegetable stock, miso paste, and almond butter and bring to a boil. Reduce the heat and simmer, covered, for about 15 minutes.

Stir in the lemon zest and season generously with salt and pepper to taste. Puree the soup until smooth, if you like, or leave as is.

Ladle into bowls and top with a nice dollop of plain yogurt and a sprinkling of chopped fresh mint.

Store, covered, in the refrigerator for up to 3 days.

*N*ot gonna lie, I'm just as excited about the bacon as I am about the cauliflower.

Roasted Cauliflower Soup with Bacon

Makes 6 servings

6 cups cauliflower florets (about 1½ pounds)

2 tablespoons olive oil, plus a little extra for drizzling

2½ teaspoons salt

1½ teaspoons pepper

2 tablespoons butter

2 cups finely sliced leeks (white and light green parts only)

1 cup finely chopped celery

1 tablespoon thyme leaves

5 slices bacon, finely chopped

4 cups chicken stock (page 99 or store-bought)

2 cups heavy cream

Preheat the oven to 400°F. Line a cookie sheet with parchment paper.

Spread the cauliflower florets across the prepared cookie sheet and drizzle with 2 tablespoons olive oil. Sprinkle with 1½ teaspoons salt and 1 teaspoon pepper. Use your hands to toss and evenly coat the cauliflower. Roast for 25 to 30 minutes, using a spatula to flip the cauliflower at the midway point to ensure even roasting, until the cauliflower is roasted through and just starting to brown. Remove the sheet from the oven and set aside.

In a large pot over medium-high heat, melt the butter. Add the leeks, celery, thyme, and bacon and cook until the vegetables have softened and the bacon is just starting to get crispy.

Add the roasted cauliflower and stir to combine. Add the chicken stock and cream and bring the soup to a boil. Reduce heat and allow the soup to simmer for 15 minutes.

Remove from the heat and transfer the soup in two or three batches to your blender to puree. (You'll need a secondary mixing bowl or bucket to hold the pureed soup while you finish the other batches. If using an immersion blender, you can puree the soup right in the pot, but you won't get as smooth a finish.) Return the soup to a large pot over medium heat to heat through before serving.

Serve the soup with a sprinkle of the remaining salt and pepper and drizzle of olive oil alongside some lovely crusty bread and butter.

Store, covered, in the refrigerator for up to 3 days. Given the cream, this soup is not the best candidate for the freezer. You could prepare the soup without the cream and freeze for up to 3 months, then add the cream after it has been thawed. But given how delicious it is I'd just eat it all.

Clearly my love for noodles outweighs my love for chicken.

Noodle Chicken Soup

Makes 6 servings

8 cups chicken stock
(page 99 or store-bought)

2 boneless, skinless chicken
breasts (about 1 pound)

½ cup peeled and chopped
carrots (½-inch pieces)

½ cup chopped celery
(½-inch pieces)

5 ounces dry spaghetti,
broken into 3-inch
lengths

2 tablespoons finely chopped
flat-leaf parsley plus more
for garnish

1 tablespoon finely chopped
dill

1 teaspoon salt

1 teaspoon pepper

(If you have already made the recipe for Basic Chicken Stock on page 99, you will have the necessary chicken and can skip this step!) In a large pot over medium-high heat, bring the chicken stock to a boil. Gently put the chicken breasts into the hot stock and reduce the heat to a simmer. Add the carrots and celery and cover. Allow the chicken to poach until cooked through, 15 to 20 minutes. Remove the chicken from the stock and set it aside to cool slightly.

Add the dry spaghetti, parsley, and dill to the stock and continue to cook until the pasta is just done. Don't leave the noodles too long or they'll get mushy.

Cut each chicken breast into small cubes, about 1 inch square. Add the chicken to the soup, season with salt and pepper and sprinkle with parsley.

Store, covered, in the refrigerator for up to 3 days. Freezing proves to be a problem because the noodles don't really stand up once thawed and reheated.

a bag of carrots never tasted so good. Well, the carrots I mean; I'm sure the bag tastes awful.

Curried Carrot Soup

Makes 6 servings

2 pounds carrots

2 tablespoons butter

2 tablespoons olive oil

1 tablespoon curry powder

1 tablespoon peeled and grated fresh ginger

2 cups peeled and finely chopped onions

1 tablespoon orange zest

8 cups chicken stock (page 99 or store-bought)

Salt and pepper

1/2 cup plain yogurt

2 tablespoons finely chopped cilantro (optional)

2 tablespoons finely chopped shelled pistachios (optional)

Peel and grate the carrots (do yourself the biggest favor and use a food processor with a grating attachment—it does all the work for you!). Set aside.

In a large pot over medium-high heat, melt the butter and olive oil. Add the curry powder, ginger, and onions and cook until the onions are soft and translucent, about 10 minutes.

Add the grated carrots and orange zest to the pot and continue to cook until the carrots start to soften, about 15 minutes. Add the chicken stock and bring the soup to a boil. Reduce the heat and allow the soup to simmer for about 15 minutes.

Remove from the heat and transfer the soup in two or three batches to your blender to puree. (You'll need a secondary mixing bowl or bucket to hold the pureed soup while you finish the other batches. If using an immersion blender, you can puree the soup right in the pot, but you won't get as smooth a finish.)

Return the soup to the pot over medium heat. Have a taste and season with salt and pepper if needed.

Serve the soup topped with a generous spoonful of yogurt and, if you like, a garnish of cilantro and chopped pistachios.

Store, covered, in the refrigerator for up to 3 days or in the freezer for up to 3 months.

I'm a big fan of cooking with parsnips in all kinds of ways, but I find that roasting them brings out their real sweetness. And if that's the secret, I think I know a few people who need to be roasted a bit longer.

Parsnip, Pear, and Blue Cheese Soup

Makes 6 servings

2 pounds parsnips, peeled and cut in 1-inch cubes

2 tablespoons olive oil

1 teaspoon salt, plus more to taste

1 teaspoon pepper, plus more to taste

2 tablespoons thyme leaves, plus additional for serving

2 tablespoons butter

½ cup peeled and finely chopped shallots

½ cup finely chopped leeks (white and light green parts only)

2 Anjou pears, peeled, cored, and chopped

6 cups chicken stock (page 99 or store-bought)

½ cup crème fraîche

½ cup crumbled blue cheese

Preheat the oven to 400°F. Line a cookie sheet with parchment paper.

Spread the parsnips across the prepared cookie sheet. Drizzle with olive oil and sprinkle with 1 teaspoon each salt and pepper and 2 tablespoons thyme leaves. Roast for 20 to 25 minutes, using a spatula to turn the parsnips over at the midway point to ensure even roasting, until the parsnips are starting to brown and are cooked through. Remove from the oven and set aside.

In a large pot over medium-high heat, melt the butter. Add the shallots, leeks, and pears and continue to cook until the leeks and shallots are soft and translucent and the pears are breaking down.

Add the roasted parsnips, chicken stock, and crème fraîche. Stir to combine. Bring the soup to a boil, then reduce the heat and allow to simmer for about 15 minutes.

Remove from the heat and transfer the soup in two or three batches to your blender to puree. (You'll need a secondary mixing bowl or bucket to hold the pureed soup while you finish the other batches. If using an immersion blender, you can puree the soup right in the pot, but you won't get as smooth a finish.)

Return the soup to the pot over medium heat. Have a taste and season with more salt and pepper if needed.

Sprinkle each serving of soup with just over a tablespoon of the crumbled blue cheese and a few thyme leaves.

Store, covered, in the refrigerator for up to 3 days. Should you want to freeze it, I suggest you don't add the crème fraîche until after you have thawed the soup. Creams don't do well in the freezer and sometimes get a little grainy once thawed and reheated.

$\mathcal{P}$retty sure I'm going to develop a scented candle based on how good this soup smells while it's cooking. I actually wanted to create a whole line of delicious savory-smelling candles, but my dog talked me out of it. She says that would mess with her head.

Mushroom Pancetta Soup

Makes 6 servings

3 tablespoons butter

½ cup peeled and finely chopped shallots

½ cup finely chopped celery

4 ounces pancetta, finely chopped

2 pounds cremini mushrooms, finely sliced

½ cup finely chopped flat-leaf parsley

1½ teaspoons salt, plus more to taste

1 teaspoon pepper, plus more to taste

6 cups chicken stock (page 99 or store-bought)

1 cup sour cream

2 tablespoons cognac

In a large pot over medium-high heat, melt the butter and sauté the shallots and celery until soft, about 10 minutes. Add the pancetta and cook for another 5 minutes, until it's just beginning to crisp. Add the sliced mushrooms, parsley, salt, and pepper and continue to cook until the mushrooms have softened and are beginning to break down, about 15 minutes.

Whisk together the chicken stock and sour cream and add it to the pot. Stir to combine. Bring the soup to a boil, then reduce the heat and allow it to simmer for about 15 minutes.

Use a large liquid measuring cup to scoop up half the soup mixture and transfer it to a blender to puree. Return it to the pot and stir to combine. Add the cognac and stir again. Have a taste and season with a little more salt and pepper if you feel it needs it.

Store, covered, in the refrigerator for several days. Should you want to freeze it, I suggest you don't add the sour cream until after you have thawed the soup.

*T*his soup is just as delicious as a fresh bagel with cream cheese and lox, but not quite as chewy. Which is a good thing, because chewy soup could be weird.

Lox and Bagel Soup

Makes 6 servings

¼ cup butter

1 cup finely sliced leeks (white and light green parts only)

1 cup finely chopped celery

½ cup peeled and finely chopped shallots

1 pound Yukon Gold potatoes, skin on, chopped in ½-inch cubes

¼ cup finely chopped fresh dill

1 teaspoon lemon zest

1 cup full-fat cream cheese

5 cups chicken stock (page 99 or store-bought)

4 ounces smoked salmon, chopped into chunks

Salt and pepper, plus sea salt for sprinkling

1 plain bagel, very thinly sliced

In a large pot over medium-high heat, melt 2 tablespoons butter. Add the leeks, celery, and shallots and cook until they begin to soften and are translucent, about 10 minutes. Add the potatoes and dill and continue to cook, stirring often, for another 10 to 15 minutes. Adjust the heat to avoid the shallots browning.

Add the lemon zest and cream cheese and stir to combine. You don't want any lumps of cream cheese, just a smooth, even coating across all the vegetables.

Add the chicken stock and stir to combine. Bring the soup to a boil, then reduce the heat and allow it to simmer for about 20 minutes, until the potatoes are soft and fully cooked.

Use a large liquid measuring cup to scoop up half the soup mixture and transfer it to a blender to puree (I like to blend only half the soup so that some chunks of potato and bits of leek and celery remain for that chowder effect). Return the puree to the pot and stir to combine. Add the chopped smoked salmon, have a taste, and season with salt and pepper if you feel it needs it.

Preheat the oven to 350°F. Melt the remaining butter in the microwave and use a pastry brush to lightly coat one side of each slice of bagel, then sprinkle with a little sea salt. Spread the bagel slices, buttered side up, across a cookie sheet lined with parchment paper, and bake in the oven for 10 to 12 minutes, until lightly browned and very crunchy.

Top each bowl of soup with some of the bagel chips and serve.

Store, covered, in the refrigerator for 2 days. Freezing isn't really an option because of the cream cheese, so eat it all up!

*G*rowing up, India's favorite meal was pasta with something we like to call sausage sauce (page 185). Now 25, she still asks me to make that dish on her birthday. I thought it might be fun to combine all those same elements to create a delicious and hearty soup for her to enjoy while waiting for her next birthday to come around.

Italian Sausage Sauce Soup

Makes 6 servings

3 mild Italian sausages, cut in ½-inch pieces

4 slices thick-cut bacon, cut in ½-inch pieces

4 cups chicken stock (page 99 or store-bought)

1 (28-ounce) can whole plum tomatoes

1 cup drained and rinsed canned chickpeas

½ cup orzo pasta

3 tablespoons butter

1 tablespoon balsamic vinegar

¼ teaspoon each salt and pepper

¼ cup finely chopped basil

Freshly grated Parmesan

In a large pot over medium-high heat, combine the sausages and bacon. Cook, stirring often, until the bacon is just starting to get a little crispy and the sausage pieces are cooked through, 10 to 15 minutes. Remove the pot from the heat and tilt it to one side to allow the excess fat to pool. Use a large spoon to spoon off and discard the fat.

Add the stock and tomatoes (with their juices) to the pot. Bring to a boil over high heat, using the back of a large spoon to help break the tomatoes down into smaller chunks. Add the chickpeas, orzo, butter, balsamic vinegar, and salt and pepper. Reduce the heat to medium-low and simmer, covered, until the orzo is tender, about 15 minutes. Add the basil and give the soup a stir.

Ladle the soup into warm bowls and serve with a generous sprinkle of grated Parmesan.

Store, covered, in the refrigerator for up to 3 days or in the freezer for up to 3 months.

13 USELESS FACTS
You Might Not Know about Me

1. I can't sing worth a damn. I'll gladly help you carry your bags, but please don't ask me to carry a tune.

2. If I had a uniform, it would include a blue striped shirt. I just can't say no to a blue stripe. On pillows, on chairs, or on my back.

3. I am kind of obsessed with blueberries and oatmeal. Big, fat fresh blueberries with steel-cut oats and probably way too much brown sugar (I also like large-flake rolled oats, but never instant—blech!).

4. I adore paper goods and ribbon! I have a large cupboard in my office filled with ribbons of every color and reams of wrapping paper for every occasion. I love a beautifully wrapped gift almost as much as the gift itself, which leads me to number 5 . . .

5. I LOVE presents. Some people are uncomfortable opening presents; I am not one of those people. I also love to give them as much as I love to receive them, and I take a lot of pride in trying to select what I hope is the perfect gift for my friends and family.

6. When I swim, I don't like to get my hair wet.

7. I'm a bath person, not so much a shower person. Nothing puts my mind and weary body at ease after a long day quite like a hot bath before bed. For some reason, I also have a habit of running the bathwater way too hot, causing me to emerge from the tub looking like a giant cooked lobster.

8. I have unusually long toes and consequently very good balance.

9. My favorite movie of all time is *Out of Africa* starring Meryl Streep and Robert Redford. I've lost count of how many times I've watched it, but whatever the number, it's not enough.

10. I will always, always prefer a real phone to a cell phone. I still call all my friends on their land lines, so when it rings, they know it's either me or someone taking a survey.

11. I prefer white wine (a big buttery California Chardonnay, specifically) to red wine, but sometimes a strong margarita (no ice and no salt on the rim) is the better option.

12. I like to go to bed early; I'm pretty sure most eight-year-olds stay up later than me.

13. We once had a dog named Carter who appeared in a Viagra commercial that was filmed in our house.

GREEN WITH ENVY

SALADS

Reviewing this chapter, you might assume I'm not a fan of lettuce. Don't get me wrong, I love the leaves! I could eat my own weight in arugula, kale, or spinach, and I've never said no to a wedge of iceberg or even the dreaded frisée (apologies to all frisée lovers, but honestly, come on). I well and truly believe that one of the finer things in life is a pile of freshly picked greens with a little squeeze of lemon and a good sprinkle of salt.

But when it comes to making salads, I'm all about the other things. Those other things—like creamy avocado, buttery breadcrumbs, spicy radish, or salty smoked bacon—are what make a salad interesting to both your stomach and your eyes. Maybe that's why we "dress" salads. The different textures, shapes, and flavors that all those delicious extra bits provide can really complete an outfit.

*P*eople say you shouldn't discuss politics or religion at the dinner table. Based on all the varying opinions on potato salad, you probably shouldn't bring that up either. I'm not sure if you're for boiled eggs or against them, but surely, people, we can agree on pickles. I mean, honestly, didn't we all grow up with pickles in the potato salad?

Old-School Potato Salad

Makes 6 side servings

2 pounds new potatoes

6 eggs

½ cup chopped gherkin pickles (½-inch pieces)

¼ cup mayonnaise

¼ cup sour cream

2 tablespoons finely chopped dill

2 tablespoons finely chopped chives

1 tablespoon grainy Dijon mustard

1 tablespoon apple cider vinegar

1 teaspoon salt

½ teaspoon pepper

Place the potatoes in a large pot of water over high heat. Bring to a boil, then reduce the heat to a simmer and allow them to cook until fork-tender, about 15 minutes. Drain the potatoes and allow them to rest. When cool enough to handle, cut the potatoes in half and put them in a large serving bowl.

Fill a medium saucepan half full with water and place it over high heat. When the water is at a full boil, use a spoon to gently lower the eggs into it, one at a time. Allow the eggs to boil for 10 minutes.

Remove the eggs from the heat and carefully drain off the boiling water. Place the saucepan under the tap and allow cold water to run on the eggs for several minutes. Move the pan to the counter and let the eggs rest in the cool water for about 15 minutes.

Take an egg and lightly tap both ends on the edge of the sink, cracking the shell. Then gently roll the egg along the counter to crack the sides of the shell. Hold the egg under running cold water while you peel off the shell. Once all the shell has been removed, give the egg a little shake to remove any excess water and place it on a cutting board. Repeat with the remaining eggs.

Cut each egg in half and place it in the bowl with the potatoes. Add the chopped gherkin pickles and toss to combine.

In a small bowl, whisk together the mayonnaise, sour cream, dill, chives, mustard, vinegar, salt, and pepper. Dress the salad and gently toss to combine. Season with more salt and pepper to taste.

Place the salad, covered, in the refrigerator for at least 1 hour prior to serving. Store, covered, in the refrigerator for up to 3 days.

*C*lose your eyes and imagine the juice of a ripe nectarine dribbling down your chin, the faint smell of warm earth on tomatoes, the easygoing effort of shelling peas, and the lingering perfume of fresh mint on your hands. Summer tastes good.

If Summer Were a Salad

Makes 6 servings

6 nectarines, quartered and cut in ¼-inch slices

1 cup fresh English peas

2 cups (1 pint) cherry tomatoes, halved

1 cup finely sliced watermelon radishes

1 cup finely sliced mint

¼ cup finely sliced basil

3 tablespoons sunflower oil

1 tablespoon white wine vinegar

1 teaspoon Dijon mustard

1 teaspoon granulated sugar

½ teaspoon salt

¼ teaspoon pepper

1 cup pea shoots (a big handful)

In a large serving bowl, combine the nectarine slices, peas, tomatoes, radishes, mint, and basil and gently toss.

In a small bowl, whisk together the oil, vinegar, mustard, sugar, salt, and pepper. Dress the salad and gently toss again. Season with more salt and pepper to taste. Top the salad with a big handful of pea shoots and serve.

This salad is best served the same day, but stored, covered, in the refrigerator, it's still pretty yummy the next day (if you don't mind the pea shoots being a little limp).

This is a very popular French salad. They serve some kind of version of it all over France. I heard that the French optometrists are circulating a petition to have it abolished.

Nutty Citrus Carrot Salad

Makes 6 side servings

1½ pounds carrots

1 cup walnuts

¼ cup finely chopped flat-leaf parsley

2 tablespoons orange juice

1 tablespoon orange zest

2 tablespoons olive oil

1 teaspoon granulated sugar

1 teaspoon Dijon mustard

1 teaspoon salt

½ teaspoon pepper

Preheat the oven to 350°F. Line a cookie sheet with parchment paper.

Wash, peel, and trim the carrots before you grate them. You can use a stand grater to grate all of the carrots by hand, but I much prefer to use my food processor, which kindly does the job in a matter of seconds. Place the grated carrots in a large serving bowl.

Spread the walnuts across the prepared cookie sheet and bake for about 10 minutes, until they are lightly toasted and fragrant. Remove from the oven and allow to cool slightly before roughly chopping the nuts with a large knife. Sprinkle the nuts and parsley over the carrots.

In a small bowl, whisk together the orange juice, zest, olive oil, sugar, mustard, salt, and pepper. Dress the salad and toss to combine.

Store, covered, in the refrigerator for up to 3 days.

*E*very year, my dad and his buddies go on a fishing trip to Haida Gwaii. If it goes well, I end up with a freezer full of salmon. If it goes really well, I also end up with a pantry full of canned smoked salmon. Then I make this salad and things go even better.

French Lentils and Fennel Salad

Makes 6 servings

1 cup dried French lentils

3 cups water

1 teaspoon salt

1 cup thinly sliced fennel, about 1 bulb

1 can smoked salmon, drained (about 1 cup)

¼ red onion, peeled and very thinly sliced

1 cup finely chopped flat-leaf parsley

2 tablespoons finely chopped dill

2 tablespoons olive oil

2 tablespoons red wine vinegar

Zest of 1 lemon

1 teaspoon salt

½ teaspoon pepper

Place the lentils in a sieve and rinse them under cold running water for a minute or two. Combine the lentils, 3 cups water, and salt in a large pot over high heat. Bring to a boil, then reduce heat and allow the lentils to simmer, covered, for about 30 minutes, until tender. Drain and set aside.

Trim the fennel stalks from the bulb and cut it in half. Using a very sharp knife or a mandoline slicer set on the thinnest setting, carefully cut the fennel into very thin slices.

Place the lentils, fennel slices, smoked salmon, red onions, parsley, and dill in a large serving bowl. Use a large spoon to gently toss to combine.

In a small bowl, whisk together the remaining ingredients, then pour over the salad and toss again. You may wish to season with a little more salt and pepper to suit your taste.

Store, covered, in the refrigerator for up to 3 days (perfect for your packed lunch the next day).

This salad covers all the bases . . . crunchy, crisp, creamy, and tender.

Little Gem with Breadcrumb Dust

Makes 6 side servings

2 tablespoons butter

½ cup panko breadcrumbs

1 teaspoon salt, plus a little more for seasoning breadcrumbs

1 cup buttermilk

½ cup crème fraîche

2 teaspoons lemon zest

¼ cup finely chopped chives

1 tablespoon thyme leaves

½ teaspoon pepper

6 heads Little Gem lettuce, halved (see note)

½ cup finely sliced French breakfast radishes

In a medium saucepan over medium heat, melt the butter. Add the breadcrumbs and stir to coat. Continue to stir until the breadcrumbs begin to brown and toast, 3 to 4 minutes. Remove from the heat and sprinkle lightly with salt. Set aside to cool.

In a small bowl, whisk together the buttermilk, crème fraîche, lemon zest, chives, thyme, 1 teaspoon salt, and pepper.

On a large serving platter, lay the Little Gem lettuce halves cut side up and slightly overlapping.

Spoon the buttermilk dressing over the lettuce halves, sprinkle with the buttery breadcrumbs, and top with sliced radishes. Sprinkle a little more salt and pepper on the radishes and serve immediately.

You can make the dressing for this salad a day or two in advance and store, covered, in the refrigerator.

PSSST . . . *If you're having a hard time finding Little Gem lettuce, you can substitute with regular romaine. If so, remove the larger outer leaves on the romaine, leaving the more delicate inner bits.*

*W*hile this salad loves making dinner plans with a protein, it's also pretty comfortable having lunch on its own.

Broccoli Ricotta Hazelnut Salad

Makes 6 side servings

8 cups broccoli florets (about 1 pound)

3 cloves garlic, peeled and finely chopped

1 teaspoon sea salt

2 tablespoons olive oil

¼ cup white wine

1 cup orzo pasta

½ cup hazelnuts

1 tablespoon finely chopped tarragon

½ cup ricotta

1 teaspoon salt

½ teaspoon pepper

Preheat the oven to 400°F. Line a cookie sheet with parchment paper.

Spread the broccoli florets across the prepared cookie sheet and sprinkle with the chopped garlic and sea salt. Drizzle with olive oil, then use your hands to toss the broccoli to ensure it's evenly coated. Roast for 10 to 12 minutes, until the broccoli is just starting to crisp around the edges. Remove from the oven and set aside to cool.

Place the white wine in a large serving bowl and set aside.

In a medium pot over high heat, prepare the orzo following the cooking instructions on the package. Once done, drain the orzo and add it to the serving bowl with wine. Stir to combine and let it sit for a bit to allow the pasta to absorb the white wine.

In a small saucepan over medium heat, toast the hazelnuts until fragrant and starting to brown, about 5 minutes. Remove from the heat and allow them to cool slightly before chopping. Set aside.

To the serving bowl with orzo, add the roasted broccoli, hazelnuts, and tarragon. Crumble the ricotta over the top and toss to combine. Season with salt and pepper and toss again.

Store, covered, in the refrigerator for up to 3 days.

I realize this recipe seems a little simplistic, but sometimes the best things are. The crunch and heat of this salad make it a great side to pretty much any summer meal. The true secret, of course, lies in the quality of your watermelon. I've tasted my fair share and find the organic ones have the most flavor. If you're desperate to complicate things a little, consider adding some cubes of avocado at the last minute. The crunchy-smooth thing is pretty great.

Watermelon and Feta Salad with Lime

Makes 6 side servings

1 small seedless watermelon, chopped (1-inch cubes)

½ cup torn mint leaves

2 teaspoons lime zest

1 teaspoon chili flakes

½ teaspoon salt

½ cup feta

1 tablespoon honey

In a large bowl, combine the watermelon, mint, lime zest, chili flakes, and salt. Crumble the feta over top of the watermelon and gently toss to combine. Drizzle with honey and serve.

This salad is best served the same day, when the watermelon is super-crunchy and fresh.

his salad reminds me of being a child again, when all my meals were conveniently cut up into bite-sized pieces—but it's infinitely better now that I can put wine in my sippy cup.

Clubhouse Chopped Salad

Makes 4 to 6 servings

2 boneless, skin-on chicken breasts

¼ cup olive oil

Salt and pepper

6 slices bacon

4 eggs

1½ cups halved grape tomatoes

1 large avocado, pitted and chopped

1 cup cubed Monterey Jack (½-inch cubes)

1 head romaine lettuce, finely chopped

¼ cup finely chopped chives

2 tablespoons apple cider vinegar

2 tablespoons honey

1 tablespoon grainy Dijon mustard

1½ teaspoons salt

1 teaspoon pepper

Preheat the oven to 375°F. Line two cookie sheets with parchment paper.

Place the chicken breasts, skin side up, on one of the prepared cookie sheets. Drizzle with 1 tablespoon olive oil and a generous sprinkle of salt and pepper. Bake for 25 to 30 minutes, until the chicken is firm to the touch and turning golden brown. Remove from the oven and allow to cool for 10 minutes before removing the skin and cutting the chicken into pieces. Set aside.

Lay the six slices of bacon side by side on the other prepared cookie sheet and bake for 15 to 20 minutes, using tongs to turn the bacon over at the halfway point, until the bacon is cooked through and crispy around the edges. Once done, remove from the oven and use the tongs to transfer the bacon to some paper towel to absorb the excess oil, then cut it into pieces. Set aside.

Bring a small pot of water to a boil over high heat. Use a spoon to gently lower the eggs into the boiling water and allow them to cook for 10 minutes. Remove the pot from the heat, drain the hot water, and refill the pot with very cold tap water to help cool the eggs. Allow them to sit in the cool water for about 10 minutes before shelling and chopping them.

Place the chopped eggs, chicken, and bacon in a large serving bowl. Add the tomatoes, avocado, cheese, lettuce, and chives.

In a small bowl, whisk the remaining olive oil together with the vinegar, honey, mustard, salt, and pepper, and pour over the salad. Use two large spoons to toss the salad and serve.

This salad is best served the same day, as the romaine will soften up once dressed.

This is a super-easy salad to pull together. Should you want to make it even easier, consider buying a jar of roasted red peppers instead of roasting your own. If you want to make it easier still, consider just ordering takeout.

Green Bean, Snow Pea, and Red Pepper Salad

Makes 6 servings

1 pound green beans, stems removed, cut in 3-inch pieces

1 (6-ounce) bag snow peas, trimmed and halved

1 red pepper

1 cup drained and rinsed canned chickpeas

2 tablespoons black sesame seeds

2 tablespoons soy sauce

1 tablespoon sesame oil

1 tablespoon rice wine vinegar

1 tablespoon honey

1 tablespoon peeled and grated fresh ginger

1 teaspoon sriracha

Salt and pepper

1 tablespoon finely chopped cilantro

Bring a large pot of salted water to a boil over high heat. Gently lower the trimmed green beans in the boiling water and allow them to cook for 2 to 3 minutes, until a lovely bright green. Remove the beans from the heat and drain off the water, leaving the beans in the pot. Place the pot under very cold running water for several minutes. Allow the beans to sit until they have cooled, then drain again.

Preheat the oven to broil on high. Line a cookie sheet with parchment paper. Place the whole red pepper on the prepared cookie sheet and broil for 12 to 15 minutes, turning every 3 to 5 minutes to make sure it is evenly charred all over.

Remove from the oven and transfer the pepper to a sealed paper bag. Allow to sit and steam for 5 minutes before removing from the bag. Use a knife to remove the skin and discard. Slice the pepper into ¼-inch slices.

Place the blanched green beans, snow peas, red peppers, chickpeas, and sesame seeds in a large serving bowl. Using a large spoon, toss to combine.

In a small bowl, whisk together the soy sauce, sesame oil, vinegar, honey, ginger, and sriracha. Dress the salad and toss to combine. Season with salt and pepper to taste and toss again. Sprinkle the salad with chopped cilantro before serving.

Store, covered, in the refrigerator for up to 3 days.

*K*ale and quinoa . . . remember when no one had even heard of them? Can vegetables and grains feel smug?

Kale, Quinoa, and Radish Salad

Makes 6 servings

½ cup quinoa, uncooked

¾ cup water

1½ teaspoons salt

5 cups baby kale

1½ cups thinly sliced radishes

½ cup pumpkin seeds

3 tablespoons olive oil

1 tablespoon fresh lemon juice

1 tablespoon Dijon mustard

½ teaspoon pepper

In a small pot over high heat, combine the quinoa, water, and ½ teaspoon salt and bring to a boil. Place the lid on, reduce the heat, and allow to simmer for 15 minutes. Remove from the heat and allow quinoa to sit for several minutes before fluffing with a fork. Set aside to cool.

In a large serving bowl, combine the baby kale, radishes, pumpkin seeds, and quinoa and toss to combine.

In a small bowl, whisk together the olive oil, lemon juice, mustard, remaining 1 teaspoon salt, and pepper. Dress the salad and toss again.

This salad is best served the same day unless you choose to make it with a heartier kale like Black or Tuscan, which has a much stronger leaf and won't break down as easily when dressed. If using, make sure to use a large knife to remove the thick, bony spines from each leaf before cutting or tearing them into bite-sized pieces.

*C*ouscous, the grain so good they named it twice.

Zucchini and Couscous Salad

Makes 6 servings

1 red pepper

½ cup uncooked couscous

½ cup pine nuts

2 medium zucchini, thinly sliced

½ cup finely chopped sun-dried tomatoes

1 cup finely chopped basil

½ cup finely chopped mint

¼ cup fresh lemon juice

⅓ cup olive oil

1 tablespoon Dijon mustard

1 teaspoon Herbes de Provence

1½ teaspoons salt

1 teaspoon pepper

Preheat the oven to broil on high. Line a cookie sheet with foil. Place the oven rack just above the center point of the oven, as you don't want the cookie sheet too close to the broiler, which could char the pepper before it is actually roasted through.

Lay the pepper on its side on the prepared cookie sheet and place under the broiler. Use your tongs to turn the pepper every 5 minutes or so until it is roasted and charred, about 15 minutes. Remove the roasted pepper from the oven, place it in a paper bag, and fold the top to close it. Allow the pepper to steam for about 15 minutes.

Remove the pepper from the bag and use a small knife to scrape away the skin. Now that it has steamed, the skin should come away very easily. Slice the pepper open, remove the stem and the remaining seeds, and cut into thin slices. Transfer to a large serving bowl.

Make the couscous following the package instructions. The ½ cup uncooked couscous should produce about 2 cups cooked. Allow to cool.

In a small saucepan over medium heat, toast the pine nuts until golden brown, about 5 minutes. Make sure to shake the pan frequently to turn and evenly toast them. Transfer the nuts to a small plate or bowl to cool.

Using a sharp knife or a food processor, thinly slice the zucchini into disks.

Add the couscous, pine nuts, sliced zucchini, sun-dried tomatoes, basil, and mint to the serving bowl with the peppers. Using a large spoon, toss to combine.

In a small bowl, whisk together the lemon juice, olive oil, mustard, Herbes de Provence, salt, and pepper. Dress the salad and toss to combine.

The dressing can be made a day ahead. Once dressed, the salad can be stored, covered, in the refrigerator for up to 3 days.

KNOW YOUR LIMIT

I hope you didn't buy this book expecting to find a recipe for mushroom lasagna. If you did, you're going to be disappointed. I suggest you buy Biba Caggiano's book, *Italy al Dente*. She has a wonderful recipe for mushroom lasagna, a recipe so good you'll want to make it again and again. Unless, like me, you attempt to make it for friends while violently ill and running a crazy-high temperature. If that happens, and you're anything like me—a stubborn perfectionist who would rather grow a tail than be considered a flake who cancels plans—you will probably try to push through and force yourself to complete the task as you weave around the kitchen in a state of delirium, mumbling, "You can do this, you got this." And at some point, a spouse or loved one might step in and force you to set aside the dish so they can take you to the hospital where you will discover you are deathly ill with pneumonia.

A little over a week later—once all the medication has taken effect and food is just starting to sound appealing—you might pull yourself out of bed and cough and wheeze all the way down to the kitchen. Once you get there, you'll no doubt use what little strength you have left to open the refrigerator, only to be confronted with the whiff of an unbaked mushroom lasagna. And that, my friends, is what is commonly referred to as a turning point. Or, perhaps more accurately, a stomach-turning point. It's also the reason you won't find a mushroom lasagna in this book, in my life, or in a ten-mile radius surrounding me. Just typing the words *mushroom lasagna* still makes me queasy.

I have no one to blame but myself for the whole fiasco, but fortunately I didn't come away from the experience empty-handed. I learned some valuable things about life, friends, cooking, and my apparent stamina.

1. Know your limit, work within it. If life has thrown you a curveball and things are stressful or you feel a cold coming on, make sure to scale back. I'm not saying you have to cancel your plans and sleep in a bomb shelter, but maybe now is not the time to attempt a dish you've never made before.

2. If you must cook when you're unwell, make sure to pick a dish you already hate.

3. Know that your friends will still love you and understand if things go sideways and you have to reschedule. No doubt they'd much rather visit you at home than in the hospital.

4. Lastly and most importantly: don't let the passion you have for the thing that brings you joy be the thing that takes the joy out of your passion—like the avid runner who ends up with two bum knees or the scholar who never takes his head out of a book. Remember that it's okay to take your eye off the target every once and a while so you don't lose sight of all the good things that surround you right now.

JUST BE HOME IN TIME IN TIME FOR . . .

DINNER

There was a time in my life when I didn't mind fussing over dinner, whether it was a weeknight meal or a special celebration with friends. Clearly I was a much younger person then with energy to spare! Since becoming a wife, mother, and business owner, that energy has all but evaporated—fortunately, my love for cooking has not. Somewhere along the way I just learned to focus on the truly important stuff. Life is hectic and exhausting, and sometimes takeout just makes sense! But more often than not, what I find I'm craving after a maddening day is the comfort of a home-cooked meal. Nothing fancy or complicated, just something honest and delicious that doesn't require a million ingredients or steps. That, in a nutshell, is the criteria for pretty much all of my recipes.

While lasagna or ribs aren't exactly reinventing the dinner wheel, my meals, like my baking, reflect my simple belief that life can be nuts on the best of days, and that a sense of the familiar (whether that's a slice of pie or a slice of meatloaf) can be a delicious reassurance that all is good.

Quiche Me You Fool

You know that friend you have who gets along with everyone? She's just so easygoing and pleasant, and nobody has an unkind word to say about her. She's available to have breakfast, lunch, or dinner with you depending on your mood. She's so darn accommodating that it's almost annoying, but you can't imagine your life without her. Okay . . . now imagine she's a quiche.

The Best and Basic Quiche
(invented by some woman named Lorraine)

Makes 1 (9-inch) quiche, 6 to 8 servings

6 slices thick-cut bacon, cut in 1-inch pieces

1 shallot, peeled and finely diced

1 recipe Flaky Quiche Pastry (see next page), prebaked

1 cup grated Gruyère

4 eggs

2 tablespoons all-purpose flour

1 cup milk

¾ cup sour cream

1 tablespoon finely chopped flat-leaf parsley

1 teaspoon salt

½ teaspoon pepper

Preheat the oven to 325°F.

In a medium skillet over medium-high heat, cook the bacon until it starts to brown. Add the shallots and cook until softened, about 5 minutes in total (if you omit the bacon, just sauté the shallots in 1 tablespoon butter). Transfer to a dinner plate lined with paper towel and pat to remove any excess fat. Spread the bacon and shallots evenly across the bottom of the prepared quiche shell. Sprinkle with the grated cheese.

In a large bowl, whisk together the eggs and flour. Add the milk, sour cream, parsley, salt, and pepper and whisk again to combine. Pour the liquid ingredients into the shell. I like to put the quiche pan atop a cookie sheet lined with parchment, as it makes it easier to get the quiche in and out of the oven and catches any spills.

Bake for 35 to 40 minutes, until the edges are set but the center remains a little wobbly. Remove from the oven and transfer to a wire rack. Allow the quiche to cool for at least 1 hour prior to removing from the pan and cutting.

Store, covered, in the refrigerator for up to 3 days. Serve cold or reheat in a 200°F oven for about 20 minutes.

Flaky Quiche Pastry

Makes 1 (9-inch) quiche shell

1½ cups all-purpose flour

½ teaspoon salt

½ cup butter, chilled and cut in 1-inch cubes

⅓ cup ice water

1 egg, lightly beaten

1 tablespoon water

Place the flour and salt in the bowl of a food processor fitted with the blade attachment. Pulse the machine a couple of times to combine. Add the cubed chilled butter to the bowl and continue to pulse until pea-sized crumbs begin to form. This happens pretty quickly, so keep your eye on it, as you don't want to over-incorporate the butter into the flour. The pea-sized chunks of butter will release steam when the quiche bakes, creating a lovely flaky pastry.

Turn the food processor on and pour the ⅓ cup ice water through the feed tube in a steady stream. As soon as the dough starts to come together, stop the machine. Remove the dough from the bowl and shape it into a disk. Wrap the disk in plastic wrap and chill in the refrigerator for at least 2 hours or overnight.

Preheat the oven to 350°F.

Remove the chilled disk of pastry from the refrigerator and place it on a lightly floured work surface. Use a rolling pin to roll from the center of the dough out toward the edges, rotating the dough every few strokes to make sure it doesn't stick to the counter. Lightly dust with more flour as needed to avoid it sticking. Continue to roll until the pastry is about ⅛ inch thick and 11 inches in diameter. Roll a pastry docker over the rolled pastry or use a fork to create random holes across the surface. The steam needs somewhere to escape when a pastry shell is blind-baked to avoid it shrinking in the pan.

Carefully fold the pastry in quarters and transfer to a 9-inch quiche pan with a removable bottom. Unfold and press the pastry into place, making sure not to stretch the pastry. Run your rolling pin across the top of the pan to cut a clean edge around the top of the pastry shell.

In a small bowl, whisk together the egg and 1 tablespoon water. Use a pastry brush to coat the inside of the pastry shell with the egg wash.

Bake for 15 minutes, until the pastry is beginning to turn a light golden brown. Remove from the oven and allow to cool before filling.

The unrolled pastry can be frozen for up to 3 months. The baked pastry shell will keep, well wrapped, in the freezer for up to 1 month.

PSSST . . . *As for the Lemon Parsley Pastry for my chicken pie, I have made this pastry in my food processor, but you can always make it by hand using a pastry cutter.*

A Slew of Fillings

There's no end to the options for filling a quiche. I've put together a little list to get you started, but have some fun and experiment to create your own. Start with my recipe for The Best and Basic (page 151) and switch up the flavors, by substituting the bacon and Gruyère in that recipe with the options suggested below. Add your alternate filling to the empty quiche shell (as you would have the bacon) and then sprinkle with your chosen cheese. Don't hesitate to mix up herbs either, but you can never go wrong with a little thyme, basil, tarragon, or dill.

ASPARAGUS AND GOAT CHEESE 2 cups chopped asparagus, woody ends removed, plus 1 cup crumbled goat cheese.

BROCCOLI, HAM, AND CHEDDAR 2 cups broccoli florets, lightly steamed, and 1 cup cubed ham, plus 1 cup grated Cheddar.

CORN, TOMATO, POBLANO CHILI, AND MONTEREY JACK 1 cup fresh corn kernels (if using frozen, make sure to thaw first) combined with 1 cup seeded and finely diced fresh tomatoes and one poblano pepper, seeded and finely diced, plus 1 cup grated Monterey Jack.

LEEK, SPINACH, AND GRUYÈRE One thinly sliced leek (white and light green parts only) sautéed with 3 cups fresh spinach leaves, plus 1 cup grated Gruyère.

POTATO, BACON, AND CHEDDAR 1 cup cubed roasted new potatoes (1-inch cubes) sautéed with six slices chopped bacon, plus 1 cup grated Cheddar.

ROASTED VEGETABLE WITH PESTO AND GOAT CHEESE Spread the bottom of the shell with ½ cup pesto (page 227), fill with 2 cups roasted vegetables (page 205), and sprinkle with 1 cup crumbled goat cheese (if you have a couple of leftover Italian sausages hanging about, I'd slice them up and throw 'em in too), and a little finely chopped fresh basil.

SWISS CHARD AND GRUYÈRE 2 cups roughly chopped fresh Swiss chard leaves, plus 1 cup grated Gruyère.

*O*riginally this dish called for only four kinds of cheese, but my love for the word *quintuple* convinced me to up the cheese quotient— that and my serious love for cheese.

Mac and Quintuple Cheese

Makes 6 to 8 servings

2 cups dry macaroni

3 cups milk

¼ cup butter plus
  2 tablespoons butter,
  melted

¼ cup all-purpose flour

1 teaspoon dried mustard

1 teaspoon salt

½ teaspoon pepper

1 cup grated smoked Gruyère

1 cup grated mozzarella

1 cup grated sharp Cheddar

1 cup grated Parmesan

½ cup cream cheese

1½ cups cherry tomatoes,
  halved

1 cup breadcrumbs

1 teaspoon cayenne pepper

Preheat the oven to 350°F. Lightly butter a 9 × 13-inch casserole dish.

Cook the macaroni according to package directions. Drain and set aside.

In a small pot over medium heat, warm the milk for 1 to 2 minutes, until hot but not boiling. Set aside.

In a large pot over medium heat, melt the ¼ cup butter until it starts to foam. Add the flour to make a roux, whisking constantly until it starts to darken slightly, 1 to 2 minutes (to ensure that the flour is cooked to avoid a doughy taste to the cheese sauce). Add the dried mustard, salt, and pepper and whisk to combine.

Slowly add the warm milk and whisk until smooth. Bring to a boil, then reduce the heat and continue to cook until the sauce has thickened, 3 to 4 minutes. You want the sauce thick enough that it will easily coat the back of a spoon. Remove the sauce from the heat and add all the grated cheeses and the cream cheese. Whisk to combine until smooth.

Add the cooked macaroni to the sauce and stir to combine until the pasta is fully coated.

Fold in the halved cherry tomatoes, then transfer the macaroni to the prepared casserole dish and use a spatula or the back of a spoon to spread it evenly across the dish.

Place the breadcrumbs, cayenne, and 2 tablespoons melted butter in a small bowl and stir to combine. Sprinkle the breadcrumb mixture evenly over the top of the macaroni.

Bake for about 30 minutes, until the breadcrumbs are golden brown and the cheese is bubbling.

Store, covered, in the refrigerator for up to 3 days, or in the freezer for up to 3 months.

O f all the reasons to own a cast-iron skillet, using it to make this halibut is my favorite. We generally cook all our fish using this method, so feel free to switch it up with some salmon or sea bass for equally delicious results.

Iron Skillet Halibut

Makes 4 servings

¼ cup all-purpose flour

1 teaspoon salt

½ teaspoon pepper

4 (6-ounce) halibut fillets
    (about 1½ inches thick)

1 tablespoon butter

1 tablespoon olive oil

Preheat the oven to 375°F.

Combine the flour, salt, and pepper in a shallow dish. Gently dredge each piece of halibut in the flour, shaking off any excess. Set aside.

In a cast-iron skillet over medium-high heat, melt the butter and olive oil until just beginning to smoke. Place each fillet skin side down and cook for 1 to 2 minutes, until the skin no longer sticks to the pan. Using large tongs, turn each fillet over and cook for another minute, then turn over again so the fillets are sitting skin side down in the pan.

Use an oven mitt to transfer the hot pan to the center rack of the pre-heated oven. Bake the halibut for 7 to 8 minutes, until the fish is opaque in the center and flakes easily with a fork.

Remove the pan from the oven and serve immediately. I think fresh halibut in season is simply delicious and doesn't need any additional marinades or sauces, but I'd never say no to a little scoop of homemade tartar sauce (page 223). Risotto Cakes (page 214) and asparagus (page 194) are great choices to accompany this dish.

Store, covered, in the refrigerator for up to 3 days.

 *(page 95)!!*

- 2 cups finely chopped sweet onion (about 1 large)
- 2 cloves garlic, peeled and finely chopped
- 2 tablespoons olive oil
- 2 pounds ground turkey breast
- 8 thick slices bacon, cut in ½-inch pieces
- 1 tablespoon chili powder
- 2 teaspoons smoked paprika
- 1 teaspoon ground cumin
- 2 teaspoons salt
- ½ teaspoon pepper
- 1 red pepper, seeded and cut in ½-inch pieces
- 1 poblano pepper, seeded and finely diced
- 1 cup frozen corn kernels
- 1 (28-ounce) can diced tomatoes
- ½ cup sun-dried tomatoes, finely chopped
- 1 (14-ounce) can pinto beans, drained
- 2 tablespoons dark brown sugar
- 1 tablespoon fancy molasses
- 2 fresh bay leaves
- 1½ cups chicken stock (page 99 or store-bought)
- Sour cream, for serving
- Sharp Cheddar (optional, for serving)
- Finely chopped cilantro, for serving
- Lime wedges (optional, for serving)

I really like chili, but I think he suspects that I only hang out with him because of his other friends, sour cream and Cheddar. I told him not to be so paranoid and that I'm crazy for him (but fingers crossed corn bread will be there . . . I've secretly got a big crush on corn bread).

Turkey Chili

Makes 6 to 8 servings

In a large pot over medium-high heat, cook the onions and garlic in the olive oil for several minutes, until they begin to soften. Add the ground turkey and chopped bacon and stir to combine. Continue to cook for 7 to 10 minutes, until the bacon and turkey are cooked through.

Add the chili powder, smoked paprika, cumin, salt, and pepper and give it a good stir to coat all the meat in the seasonings. Continue to cook for several minutes, until the spices become quite fragrant.

Add the red peppers, poblano peppers, frozen corn, diced tomatoes, sun-dried tomatoes, pinto beans, brown sugar, molasses, and bay leaves. Stir to combine and allow it to cook for several minutes. Stir in the chicken stock and bring the chili to a boil. Place the lid on the pot, reduce the heat to a simmer, and allow the chili to cook for at least 2 hours.

Serve the chili topped with a big scoop of sour cream and a sprinkle of Cheddar and cilantro (and maybe a squeeze of lime if you're feeling it).

This chili, like most, gets better as the week progresses and the flavors meld. Store, covered, in the refrigerator for 3 days. It will also keep really well in the freezer for up to 3 months.

I had to break up with fried chicken. It was proving to be too big a commitment to maintain our relationship. He wanted me standing over a hot stove all day, attending to his every need. Then I met his cousin, chicken cutlet, who has all the same great qualities but isn't half as demanding of my time and attention. It's early, but I feel like this could really work out for us—although I imagine it's going to be a little awkward at family gatherings.

Fried Chicken for Impatient People Like Me

Makes 4 servings

1 cup self-rising flour

1 teaspoon finely chopped thyme leaves

1 teaspoon salt, plus a little more for seasoning

½ teaspoon pepper

½ teaspoon onion powder

¼ teaspoon garlic powder

¼ teaspoon chili flakes

¼ teaspoon smoked paprika

2 cups sour cream

4 boneless, skinless chicken breasts (about 2 pounds)

½ cup vegetable oil

2 lemon wedges

Combine the flour, thyme, salt, pepper, onion powder, garlic powder, chili flakes, and paprika in a shallow bowl (I like to use glass pie plates) and stir to combine. Place the sour cream in another shallow bowl; if it's on the thicker side, give it a good stir to help loosen it up.

Place a chicken breast between two sheets of parchment and use a kitchen mallet to pound it down to ¼ inch thick. (If you don't have a mallet, consider using the underside of a cast-iron skillet. A couple of good whacks should do the trick and work out any pent-up frustrations you may have.) Repeat with the remaining chicken breasts.

Dredge a chicken breast in the flour mixture. Gently shake off any excess and then dredge the chicken in the sour cream to coat all sides. Again, try to remove any excess before placing the chicken in the flour once more to coat. Repeat with the remaining chicken breasts.

In a large skillet, heat the oil over medium-high heat. Working in batches of two, cook each chicken breast for about 4 minutes per side, until crispy and a lovely golden brown. Make sure to adjust the heat as needed to avoid burning the cutlets.

Use tongs to transfer the cooked chicken to a paper towel–lined cookie sheet to help absorb any excess fat. Give each cutlet another sprinkle of salt and a squeeze of lemon, and serve.

Store the chicken, covered, in the refrigerator for up to 3 days.

 *(page 94)!!*

*M*aking a great roast chicken is, in my view, a necessary life skill. Much like being able to change a flat tire or perform the Heimlich maneuver, having this recipe in your arsenal will prove to be life saving time and time again. Roast one (or two, depending on the crowd) for Sunday dinner and then use the leftovers all week in sandwiches, salads, or pasta.

Roasted Chicken with Dijon Herb Butter

Makes 1 chicken, 4 servings

1 (4-pound) roasting chicken

Salt and pepper

1 small lemon, quartered

1 recipe Dijon Herb Butter (page 229), cut in 6 round pieces

2 tablespoons olive oil

Dressing

3 tablespoons olive oil

1 tablespoon fresh lemon juice

1 tablespoon grainy Dijon mustard

½ teaspoon salt

¼ teaspoon pepper

5 to 6 cups baby arugula, washed and dried

Preheat the oven to 400°F.

Rinse the chicken thoroughly and pat it dry all over with paper towel to remove any excess moisture; this will help ensure the bird gets a nice crispy skin when roasting. I like to allow the bird to come to room temperature before cooking.

Place the chicken in a 9 × 13-inch roasting pan and tuck the wings under the body.

Generously season the inside of the cavity with salt and pepper, then place the lemon quarters inside. Gently lift the breast skin of the bird and place two rounds of the Dijon herb butter under the skin atop each breast (using four rounds of butter in total). I like to use the back side of a spoon to help me lift the skin, being careful to take my time so as to not tear it. Once the butter is in place, use some kitchen twine to tie the legs together in a simple bow.

Rub the outside of the bird with the olive oil and generously season with more salt and pepper.

Place the chicken in the oven and roast for 15 to 20 minutes per pound (60 to 80 minutes for this 4-pound bird) or until the juices run clear when you make a little cut between the thigh and leg. Baste the bird with juices every 15 minutes until done.

Remove from the oven and place the last two pieces of Dijon butter atop the chicken, then tent with foil and allow to rest for about 15 minutes.

Make the dressing: Place all the ingredients for the dressing in a small liquid measuring cup and whisk to fully combine. (I also like to use a leftover jam jar to mix salad dressings; just put everything in the jar, make sure the lid is on tight, and give it a good shake.)

Spread the arugula across a serving platter and gently toss with the dressing. Place the warm chicken atop the arugula and serve! (You can also carve the bird beforehand and place the pieces atop the arugula, but I think it's a little more fun to carve the bird at the table, and—bonus!—the salad gets smothered in its lovely juices.)

PSSST . . . *Follow these easy steps and I guarantee you a delicious, moist bird! For the mechanical lessons and choking stuff check out YouTube.*

 *(page 95)!!*

I chose to build this recipe as a traditional pie, but it would work just as well as a pot pie, meaning you fill a 9 × 13-inch casserole dish with the chicken filling and just top with a lovely layer of pastry, saving you time and effort. Either option is delicious, but best not served à la mode.

Chicken Pie

Makes 1 (9-inch) pie, 6 to 8 servings

4 bone-in, skin-on chicken breasts (about 3 pounds)

4 teaspoons olive oil

4 teaspoons salt

1½ teaspoons pepper

2 tablespoons butter

1½ cups peeled and finely chopped onions

1½ cups chopped celery (½-inch pieces)

1½ cups peeled and chopped carrots (½-inch pieces)

2 cups chopped white mushrooms (½-inch pieces)

1 tablespoon thyme leaves

2 tablespoons finely chopped flat-leaf parsley

¼ cup all-purpose flour

1 cup chicken stock (page 99 or store-bought)

½ cup milk

1 cup frozen peas

Zest of 1 lemon

1 recipe Lemon Parsley Pastry (see below)

Preheat the oven to 425°F. Line a cookie sheet with parchment paper.

Place the chicken breasts on the prepared cookie sheet. Sprinkle the chicken generously with the olive oil, 2 teaspoons salt, and 1 teaspoon pepper. Place in the oven on the center rack and bake for 25 to 30 minutes, until the chicken is firm to the touch. Remove the chicken from the oven and set aside to cool.

Once the chicken is cool enough to handle, remove the skin and bones from each breast and cut the meat into 1-inch pieces. Set aside.

In a large pot over medium heat, melt the butter and add the onions. Cook until the onions are soft and translucent, about 10 minutes. Adjust your heat to avoid browning the onions. Add the celery, carrots, and mushrooms to the pot and continue to cook until they soften, about another 10 minutes. Add 2 teaspoons salt, ½ teaspoon pepper, thyme, parsley, and flour and stir well to coat all the vegetables. Reduce the heat and continue to stir for 2 to 3 minutes more.

Add the chicken stock and give a good stir to remove any bits of flour stuck to the bottom of the pot. Add the milk and stir again. You should have a nice thick sauce coating all your vegetables. Add the frozen peas, lemon zest, and chopped chicken and stir to combine. Set aside.

Preheat the oven to 375°F.

Remove one of the chilled disks of pastry from the refrigerator and place on a lightly floured work surface. Use a rolling pin to roll from the center of the dough out toward the edges, rotating the dough every few strokes to make sure it doesn't stick to the counter. Lightly dust with more flour as needed. Roll until the pastry is about ⅛ inch thick

Follow me

1 egg

1 tablespoon water

PSSST . . . *You can also freeze the pie unbaked. To bake from frozen, just add an additional 15 to 20 minutes to the baking time.*

and 11 inches in diameter. Carefully fold the pastry in quarters and transfer to a 9-inch pie dish. Unfold and press the pastry into place.

Fill the pastry shell with the prepared chicken filling. Set aside.

Remove the second disk of pastry from the refrigerator and repeat the rolling process, then place the rolled pastry on top of the pie filling. Trim with a knife or kitchen shears to leave about a 1-inch overhang. Roll and tuck the overhang back under the edge of the pie shell.

Use your index finger to push finger-sized sections of dough from the inside edge of the pie dish. Use the index finger and thumb on your opposite hand to pinch each section into a point. Continue this process all around the pie shell. Use a small paring knife to create four vents in the top of the pie, each about 2 inches long.

In a small bowl, whisk together the egg and water and use a pastry brush to coat the top of the pie shell.

Place the pie in the preheated oven and bake for 40 to 45 minutes, until the pastry is a lovely golden brown.

Store covered in the refrigerator for up to 3 days, or in the freezer for up to 1 month.

Lemon Parsley Pastry
Makes enough pastry for 1 double-crust pie

2½ cups all-purpose flour

2 tablespoons finely chopped flat-leaf parsley

Zest of 1 lemon

1 teaspoon salt

1 cup butter, chilled and cut in 1-inch cubes

½ cup ice water

PSSST . . . *I've opted to make this in the food processor, but you can always make it by hand using a pastry cutter if time allows.*

Place the flour, parsley, lemon zest, and salt in the bowl of a food processor fitted with the blade attachment. Pulse to combine.

Add the cubed chilled butter to the bowl and pulse until pea-sized crumbs begin to form. Keep your eye on it, as you don't want to over-incorporate the butter into the flour. The pea-sized chunks of butter will release steam when the pie bakes, creating a lovely flaky pastry.

Turn the food processor on and pour the ice water through the feed tube in a steady stream. As soon as the dough starts to come together, stop the machine.

Remove the dough from the bowl, divide it in two, and gently shape each piece into a disk. Wrap each disk in plastic wrap and chill in the refrigerator for at least 2 hours or overnight.

Store wrapped in the refrigerator for up to 3 days, or in the freezer for up to 1 month.

Roasted Vegetables

1 small eggplant, skin removed and flesh cut in 1-inch cubes

1 yellow and 1 red pepper, seeded and cut in 1-inch pieces

1 medium zucchini, cut in 1-inch pieces

2 tablespoons olive oil

Generous sprinkle of salt and pepper

1 teaspoon dried Italian seasoning

Chicken

3 eggs, lightly beaten

1½ teaspoons salt

½ cup all-purpose flour

1 teaspoon pepper

2 cups breadcrumbs

1 cup grated Parmesan

6 bone-in, skinless chicken breasts

2 to 3 tablespoons olive oil

1 medium onion, peeled and finely chopped

2 cups orzo pasta

4 cups chicken stock (page 99 or store-bought)

½ cup red wine

2 cups strained tomatoes

½ cup sliced black olives

Zest of 1 lemon

6 slices smoked mozzarella

I created this recipe with Paul in mind. Not the chicken part . . . the one-pot part. It was all in the hopes he might actually use only one pot. Paul is a great cook, and after I've spent a long day at the bakery, I am so grateful when he makes dinner. But somehow, in Paul's hands, the simplest of dishes requires the use of every pot and pan we own. In our house, if you do the cooking you don't have to do the cleaning, so there I am after a complex meal of poached eggs on toast wondering why the hell I'm washing a Bundt pan, chopsticks, and our salad spinner.

One-Pot Chicken Parm

Makes 6 servings

Make the roasted vegetables: Preheat the oven to 425°F. Line a cookie sheet with parchment paper.

Spread the eggplant, peppers, and zucchini across the prepared cookie sheet. Sprinkle with olive oil, salt and pepper, and Italian seasoning. Use your hands to gently toss and coat all the vegetables.

Roast the vegetables for 20 to 30 minutes, until they are fully cooked and starting to get nice and toasty all around the edges. I like to use a metal spatula to give the vegetables a flip or two at the halfway point. Once done, remove from the oven and set aside. Reduce the oven temperature to 350°F.

Make the chicken: Place the beaten eggs and ½ teaspoon salt into a shallow dish and stir. In another dish, combine the flour, 1 teaspoon salt, and pepper. In a third dish, combine the breadcrumbs and grated Parmesan. Coat a chicken breast in the flour on all sides, shaking off any excess. Now dip the breast in the egg and dredge in the breadcrumbs and cheese. Set the coated chicken on a platter and repeat with the remaining breasts.

In a large skillet set over medium-high, heat about 2 tablespoons olive oil. Working in batches, add the chicken breasts to the pan and cook

Just a wee bit more

until golden brown. Use tongs to turn the chicken and repeat, about 5 to 7 minutes per side. You may need to add a smidge more oil to the pan between batches. Once done, place the chicken on a large plate or platter and set aside. Don't stack them, as you don't want them to steam against each other and make your lovely crispy crust fall off.

Add the chopped onions to the pan and sauté until translucent and soft, 3 to 4 minutes. Add the orzo and continue to cook while stirring for another 2 minutes. Add the chicken stock, wine, strained tomatoes, olives, roasted vegetables, and lemon zest to the pan and stir to combine. Gently place the chicken into the pan and allow the sauce to come up to a boil. Place the lid on the pan and transfer it to the oven for 30 to 40 minutes.

Lift the pan from the oven and remove the lid. Lay a piece of cheese atop each chicken breast. Turn the oven to broil. Place the pan under the broiler for a minute or so, until the cheese has melted and is starting to bubble. Remove the pan from the oven and serve.

Store, covered, in the refrigerator for up to 3 days.

¼ cup all-purpose flour

1 teaspoon salt, plus more to taste

½ teaspoon pepper, plus more to taste

2 pounds cubed stewing beef

6 slices thick-cut bacon, cut in ½-inch pieces

1 medium onion, peeled and finely chopped

1 leek (light green and white parts only), washed and finely chopped

2 cloves garlic, peeled and finely chopped

1 tablespoon olive oil

1 medium parsnip, peeled and cut in ½-inch pieces

3 medium carrots, peeled and cut in ½-inch pieces

5 stalks celery, cut in ½-inch pieces

1 pound cremini mushrooms, thickly sliced

1 tablespoon thyme leaves

2 teaspoons finely chopped rosemary

3 dried or fresh bay leaves

4 cups beef stock

1 cup red wine

1 cup frozen peas

1 recipe Parsley Dumplings (see below)

*I*n our house, beef stew season starts mid-September and generally runs through to March, though there are no hard and fast rules on this and certainly no penalty should you partake in a bowl in July. I just think of it as the perfect dinner on a cold winter night. If you don't feel like making dumplings, you can always spoon a nice helping of stew atop a hearty slice of lightly toasted bread.

Beef Stew with Dumplings

Makes 6 servings

Preheat the oven to 375°F.

Place the flour, salt, pepper, and stewing beef in a large resealable plastic bag. Carefully seal the bag and give it several good shakes to fully coat the beef with the flour and seasoning. Set aside.

In a large pot or Dutch oven over medium-high heat, cook the bacon for several minutes until it is just starting to brown. Add the onions, leeks, and garlic and continue to cook until they have softened and the onions are translucent, 5 to 7 minutes.

Add the olive oil to the pot and then the floured beef. Cook until the beef starts to brown, 8 to 10 minutes.

Add the parsnips, carrots, celery, mushrooms, and herbs to the pot and give it a good stir to combine. Season with salt and pepper to taste. Allow the vegetables to continue to cook for another 5 to 8 minutes, making sure to stir every so often and adjust the heat to avoid scorching the bottom of the pot.

Add the beef stock and red wine and bring the stew to a boil. Place the lid on the pot and put it in the oven for 1½ hours. You can remove the lid for the last 20 minutes if you like your sauce a little thicker.

Remove the pot from the oven, stir in the frozen peas, and spoon 12 portions of dumpling batter atop the stew. Place the lid back on and return it to the oven for about 15 minutes, until the dumplings are fluffy and cooked through.

Over you go

Store, covered, in the refrigerator for up to 3 days or in the freezer for up to 3 months. If you plan to freeze this, don't make the dumplings until you have thawed and reheated the stew.

Parsley Dumplings
Makes 12 dumplings

2 cups all-purpose flour

1 tablespoon baking powder

1 teaspoon salt

¼ cup finely chopped flat-leaf parsley

¼ cup butter, chilled

¾ cup milk

½ cup sour cream

Place the flour, baking powder, salt, and parsley in a large bowl. Use a pastry cutter to cut in the chilled butter until pea-sized crumbs form. Place the milk and sour cream in a small bowl, use a fork to quickly whisk together, and add to the dry ingredients. Continue to stir until the dough just comes together.

Make sure your stew is nice and hot from the oven before spooning 12 equal portions of the dough across the top of the stew and returning to the oven to finish cooking, as above.

Store, atop of your leftover stew, in the refrigerator for up to 3 days.

There is absolutely no point in freezing leftover lasagna in my house. That would just be a pain for Paul when he had to thaw it every night until it was gone—because he will eat it every night, until it's gone. You might have better luck saving leftovers at your house . . . just don't tell Paul where you live.

Lasagna for Paul

Makes 6 to 8 servings

Fresh Pasta (see note)

2 cups all-purpose flour

1/2 teaspoon salt

4 eggs

Béchamel Sauce

3 cups milk

3 tablespoons butter

3 tablespoons all-purpose flour

1 teaspoon salt

1/2 teaspoon grated fresh nutmeg

6 cups Gram's Spaghetti Sauce (page 186)

2 cups ricotta

3 cups grated mozzarella

1 cup grated Parmesan

Make the pasta: Place the flour and salt into a large bowl. Make a well in the center of the flour and crack the eggs into it. Use a fork to gently whisk the eggs while simultaneously pulling in the flour from the edges of the well. When the dough becomes too thick to stir with a fork, use your fingers to work in the flour. You may find there is some leftover flour depending on the size of the eggs used and the humidity. No worries.

Transfer the dough to a clean work surface and knead it for about 10 minutes, until it is shiny and smooth. If the dough still proves to be a little sticky, just sprinkle the work surface with a little flour and continue kneading until smooth. Wrap the dough in plastic wrap and allow it to rest in the refrigerator for at least 1 hour to give the gluten that has developed a chance to relax. This will make rolling the pasta a little easier on you.

Remove the dough from the refrigerator and cut it into four equal pieces. Work with one piece at a time, tightly wrapping the remaining pieces in plastic wrap so they don't dry out.

If you have a pasta machine, follow the manufacturer's instructions for rolling and cutting the dough. If you don't have a pasta machine, not to worry, as a rolling pin and some strong arms will do the trick. Lightly flour your work surface and roll each piece of dough into a large, very thin rectangle, about 7 inches wide × 20 inches long. It takes a bit of work to get the pasta thin enough when rolling by hand, but it's so worth it in the end. A good indication that the dough is thin enough is the ability to see your hand through it when it's held up to the light. You can then cut it in half to create one layer by laying the two pieces side by side in the dish.

A lil' more work to be done

Repeat with the remaining dough to create a total of four pasta layers. Set aside, making sure the layers are not touching to avoid them sticking to each other. There's no need to boil the fresh pasta before assembling the lasagna, as the moisture from the sauce will be enough to cook it in the pan (yet another reason to make sure you roll your dough thin enough). If you're using dry pasta, just follow the directions for use on the box.

Make the béchamel sauce: In a medium-sized pot over medium heat, warm the milk until hot but not yet boiling. Set aside.

In a large pot over medium heat, melt the butter until it starts to foam. Add the flour to make a roux, whisking constantly until it starts to darken slightly, 1 to 2 minutes. You want to ensure the flour is properly cooked through to avoid a doughy taste to your sauce. Slowly add the warm milk and whisk until smooth. Bring to a boil, then reduce the heat and continue to cook until the sauce has thickened, 3 to 4 minutes. You want the sauce thick enough that it will easily coat the back of a spoon. Add the salt and nutmeg and whisk again. Set aside.

Preheat the oven to 375°F.

Spread 1½ cups Gram's sauce on the bottom of a 9 × 13-inch casserole dish. Top with one layer of prepared pasta. Spread 1 cup béchamel sauce across the pasta layer and sprinkle with 1 cup ricotta and 1 cup grated mozzarella. Top with a second layer of pasta. Spread 2 more cups of Gram's sauce across the pasta and top with a third layer of pasta. Spread another 1 cup béchamel sauce across the pasta layer and sprinkle with another 1 cup ricotta and 1 cup grated mozzarella. Top with a fourth layer of pasta.

Top with 2½ cups Gram's sauce and sprinkle with 1 final cup of mozzarella and the Parmesan.

Place the casserole dish on a cookie sheet lined with parchment paper to catch any drips in the oven. Bake for about 45 minutes, until the cheesy top is a dark golden brown and the sauce is bubbling up.

Remove the lasagna from the oven and allow it to rest for at least 15 minutes prior to cutting so everything has a little time to cool down and set up. I always have a hard time abiding by this rule, even though I made it. Instead, I make a sloppy mess of my servings and inevitably burn my mouth. I guess Paul's not the only one who loves lasagna.

Seriously, this lasagna freezes beautifully, well wrapped, for up to 3 months.

PSSST . . . *I make my own lasagna noodles because I have a great pasta-making attachment for my stand mixer, but I have also made it many, many times with dry pasta and it tastes just as good. Just ask Paul.*

For those days when you're trying to consume a little less meat and a lot more veggies, this switch-up couldn't be easier. Simply follow the recipe for my traditional lasagna (page 177), but replace the meat sauce layers with a simple tomato sauce and roasted vegetables.

Roasted Vegetable Lasagna

Makes 6 to 8 servings

1 recipe Lasagna for Paul (minus Gram's Spaghetti Sauce) (page 186)

2 (28-ounce) cans whole plum tomatoes

1 recipe Roasted Veg (page 205)

3 cups grated smoked mozzarella (see note)

PSSST . . . *I opt to use a smoked mozzarella in place of regular mozzarella because I think the smokiness makes for a fantastic complement to the veggies, but if you're not a fan, then by all means stick with straight-up mozzarella.*

Follow the recipe for Lasagna for Paul (page 177) until the point of adding the meat sauce.

Preheat the oven to 375°F.

Place the canned tomatoes in a large mixing bowl and use your hands to crush them until you have a nice chunky tomato sauce. (I don't generally add salt and pepper, as I find that the seasoning on the roasted vegetables that comes later is generous enough.)

Spread 1½ cups tomato sauce and half of the roasted vegetables across the bottom of a 9 × 13-inch casserole dish (given that the roasted vegetables are a little chunky, you want to make sure that the dish is at least 2 inches deep). Top the sauce and vegetables with one layer of the prepared pasta. Spread 1 cup of béchamel sauce across the pasta layer and sprinkle with 1 cup ricotta and 1 cup smoked mozzarella. Top with another layer of pasta. Spread with 1½ cups tomato sauce and the remaining roasted vegetables and top with a third layer of pasta. Spread 1 cup béchamel sauce across the pasta layer and sprinkle with 1 cup ricotta and 1 cup smoked mozzarella. Top with another layer of pasta. Top with the remaining tomato sauce and sprinkle with 1 final cup of smoked mozzarella and the Parmesan.

Place the casserole dish on a cookie sheet lined with parchment paper to catch any drips in the oven. Bake for about 45 minutes, until the cheesy top is a dark golden brown and the sauce is bubbling up.

Remove from the oven and allow to rest for at least 15 minutes prior to cutting so everything has a little time to cool down and set up.

Store, covered, in the refrigerator for up to 5 days or tightly wrapped in the freezer for up to 3 months.

I have spent years developing a system for rating the quality of a meatloaf recipe. It's very scientific and requires a lot of math and spreadsheets. Okay . . . that's a lie. I simply apply the sandwich test. Will it also make a good sandwich the next day? Yes? Okay, people, we've got a winner.

D.G.M.

(Damn Good Meatloaf)

Makes 1 meatloaf, 6 servings

1 pound ground veal

1 pound ground pork

1 pound ground beef

1 medium onion, peeled and grated

2 eggs, lightly beaten

¼ cup tomato paste

½ cup ground breadcrumbs

¼ cup milk

1 cup grated Cheddar

1 teaspoon dried Italian seasoning

1½ teaspoons salt

½ teaspoon pepper

¼ cup ketchup for coating meatloaf

Preheat the oven to 375°F. Line a cookie sheet with parchment paper.

In a large bowl, combine the meats and gently break them up with your hands. Add the remaining ingredients except the ketchup. Again, use your hands to gently mix and bring everything together, but try not to overwork or compress the meat, which will prevent the juices from flowing and make your meatloaf tough and dry.

Shape the meat into a 5 × 10-inch log on the prepared cookie sheet. Use a pastry brush or your hands to coat the meatloaf all over with the ketchup.

Bake in the preheated oven for 1 hour or until a meat thermometer inserted in the center registers 155°F. Remove the meatloaf from the oven and allow it to rest, loosely covered with foil, for 10 minutes before serving. Serve a thick slice alongside mashed potatoes (page 212), a spoonful of roasted cherry tomatoes (page 196), and roasted zucchini (page 201) for a perfect weeknight meal.

Store, covered, in the refrigerator for up to 3 days or in the freezer for up to 1 month.

 *(page 95)!!*

I have to thank my friend Margie for this recipe, because she was kind enough to share her method. Boiling the ribs in pineapple juice first helps to tenderize the meat, which makes for the most delicious, fall-off the bone ribs! Now all you need is some Cheesy Corn Bread (page 59), Maple Baked Beans (page 213), and a big napkin to wipe your sticky fingers! I have chosen to make my own barbecue sauce, but a good store-bought one works just as well.

Pineapple Honey Ribs

Makes 6 servings

4 pounds pork spareribs (2 racks)

12 cups pure, unsweetened pineapple juice

1 recipe Honey Barbecue Sauce (page 222)

Place the ribs and pineapple juice in a large stockpot over high heat. You can place the ribs on their side and bend them around the inside of the pot to make them fit. Bring the pineapple juice to a boil, turn the heat down to low, cover, and allow the ribs to simmer for about 1½ hours.

Remove the ribs from the pineapple juice and place them in a 9 × 13-inch baking dish. Discard the juice.

Preheat the oven to 325°F.

Use a pastry brush to heavily coat the ribs on all sides with the barbecue sauce. Bake in the oven for about 1 hour, until the sauce has begun to caramelize. Pull the finished ribs from the oven, cut them into six portions, and enjoy!

PSSST . . . *You can throw the ribs onto a hot barbecue for about 10 minutes instead of baking them in the oven if it's a lovely sunny evening and you're eating outdoors. This is also a great dish to prepare in advance of entertaining, as you can boil the ribs in the juice and then store them, covered, in the refrigerator overnight until you're ready to bake or grill.*

his was always India's request for her birthday dinner (or pretty much any occasion). We are all big fans, so clearly the love for this dish is genetic. If you like it too, does that mean we're related?

Sausage Sauce for India

Makes 6 servings

1 pound Italian sausage
(about 5 sausages)

6 slices thick-cut bacon, cut
in ½-inch pieces

3 pounds Roma tomatoes

2 cups finely chopped basil

½ teaspoon salt

½ teaspoon chili flakes

1 tablespoon balsamic
vinegar

2 tablespoons tomato paste

Pasta of your choice (rigatoni
is great), for serving

Grated Parmesan, for serving

Run a small knife gently down the side of each sausage to cut through the casing. Pull back the casing and remove the ground sausage meat.

In a large skillet over medium-high heat, cook the sausage meat and bacon until browned and cooked through, 7 to 10 minutes. Use your spatula or wooden spoon to break up the sausage meat as it is cooking.

Use a large knife to quarter each tomato, remove the seeds, and finely chop in ¼-inch pieces.

Add the chopped tomatoes to the sausage and bacon and continue to cook until the tomatoes have broken down, about 15 minutes. Add the basil, salt, chili flakes, vinegar, and tomato paste and give a good stir to combine. Reduce the heat and allow the sauce to simmer for about 20 minutes.

Make a pot of your favorite pasta (I find that rigatoni catches all the sausage bits nicely), smother it in sauce, and finish with a generous sprinkle of grated Parmesan.

Store the sauce, covered, in the refrigerator for up to 3 days or in the freezer for up to 3 months.

*T*his is the spaghetti sauce I grew up on. There was never really a recipe because my mum just did her thing. And then I just did my thing. And I hope you'll just do your thing. Every time I make this sauce, it's slightly different: a little more celery, or a little less vinegar, or a smidge more meat, or somehow a zucchini sneaks its way into the blender. No worries. It's always different but always delicious, and always better the second day.

Gram's Spaghetti Sauce

Makes 10 cups, about 8 servings

1 pound lean ground beef

2 tablespoons olive oil

2 medium carrots, peeled and halved

4 stalks celery, halved

1 medium onion, peeled and quartered

1 cup water

2 (28-ounce) cans whole plum tomatoes

1 tablespoon granulated sugar

1 tablespoon balsamic vinegar

2 tablespoons butter

¼ cup tomato paste

2 tablespoons dried Italian seasoning

1½ teaspoons salt

½ teaspoon pepper

Pasta of your choice (spaghetti for us), for serving

In a large pot over medium-high heat, brown the ground beef in the olive oil, making sure to completely cook it through. Your beef should be a darkish brown and have a nice crisp on it for maximum flavor, about 7 to 10 minutes. Don't rush it, because gray ground beef isn't thoroughly cooked and doesn't taste very good.

In a blender, combine the carrots, celery, onions, and water. Blend on high until almost smooth.

Once the meat is fully browned, add the pureed vegetables, canned tomatoes, sugar, vinegar, butter, tomato paste, Italian seasoning, salt, and pepper. Stir to combine. Bring to a boil, then reduce heat, cover, and allow to simmer for at least 2 hours (the longer the better). Make sure to have a spoonful at the halfway point and adjust the seasoning accordingly.

Make a pot of your favorite pasta and toss it with a good amount of the sauce. I really like to add another big ladleful on top of each serving and a big spoonful of freshly grated Parmesan.

This sauce makes a good-sized batch and freezes really well for up to 3 months, so you may want to fill a couple of containers with leftovers and pop them in the freezer for future pasta cravings or homemade lasagna. It also stores in the refrigerator for 3 to 5 days.

*T*his dish comes with no guarantees, but I'm confident that whomever you make it for is bound to fall in love with you. Which is awesome, unless you're serving it to a crowd. Then things could get complicated.

How to Catch a Husband Lamb

Makes 4 to 6 servings

3 pounds bone-in leg of lamb

8 cloves garlic, peeled

1½ teaspoons salt

1 teaspoon pepper

½ cup Dijon mustard

1 tablespoon finely chopped flat-leaf parsley

1 tablespoon finely chopped rosemary

½ cup all-purpose flour

Preheat the oven to 350°F.

Place the lamb on a cutting board and use a small sharp knife to make eight slits across the surface area, evenly spaced. Insert a clove of garlic into each slit and press it down until level with the lamb. Generously season the outside of the lamb with the salt and pepper.

In a small bowl, combine the mustard with the parsley and rosemary. Use a pastry brush or your hands to evenly coat the entire lamb. Place the flour in a shallow baking dish or on a cookie sheet, then gently press the lamb into it on all sides to cover the mustard coating.

Place the lamb in a 9 × 13-inch baking dish and bake for about 80 minutes for medium-rare or until a meat thermometer registers 140°F to 145°F.

Remove the lamb from the oven and allow it to rest for 10 to 15 minutes before carving. This lamb makes for a perfect Sunday dinner alongside some roasted new potatoes (page 210) and green beans (page 202). You might also consider serving it with a spoonful of mint pesto (page 227) to make it even more delicious!

Store the lamb, covered, in the refrigerator for up to 3 days.

 *(page 95)!!*

SENIOR DOGS

For those of you who have my second book, *Butter Celebrates!*, you might recall the chapter that focuses on my dog Zelda's birthday. For those of you who don't have the book, Zelda in a party hat is just a smidge of all the good stuff you're missing out on.

Like so many great things that happen in life, we found Zelda when we didn't even know we were looking. For such a little dog, she arrived with a lot of baggage, and it took us quite a while to convince her she was safe and loved. I never felt the effort to win her over was a hardship, though, as I truly believe that there are few greater accomplishments than earning the trust of an animal, especially a fearful old rescue dog that had had such a tough go of it.

The best part of adopting a senior dog is getting to know them as they gradually let their guard down and reveal their true self. Over time, we discovered Zelda liked popcorn and tummy rubs. She wasn't a fan of the vacuum or bath time, and god help the mailman or the gardener if they entered her line of sight. She wasn't a young dog, and her hard life only compounded her physical problems, but like all four-legged animals, she wasn't a complainer. It's just us two-legged ones who like to gripe. The tail wagged, the toys squeaked, and she was always up for a walk, unless of course it was raining. If she even sniffed a raindrop on the horizon, she'd put the brakes on pretty hard and promptly head straight back to bed. Of all her traits, it was her insistence on sleeping on our bed every night that proved to be our favorite. Paul and I tried to keep her out, but she eventually wore us down. It really wasn't that hard—we're a couple of pushovers who grew to love the comfort and reassurance of patting her chubby little backside as we drifted off to sleep.

Sadly, our life with Zelda was cut short in the spring of 2017 when her ailments finally caught up with her. I'm not going to lie; losing Zelda really took it out of me. I truly loved that temperamental little sausage. She may have had a tough outer shell, but all those who were patient enough soon discovered that beneath it hid the most loving heart.

As much as I missed Zelda, I also missed our life with Zelda. The daily routines, the companionship, and the responsibility of being needed. But most of all, I missed our walks. Nothing forces you to get out and stay connected to the world around you more than your dog's full bladder. Those walks provided me with time to reflect or say hi to my neighbors, and every night after dinner, an opportunity to catch up with Paul.

Emotionally I wasn't ready for another dog, but physically I was. So when our daughter, India, showed me a picture on the Internet of a tiny old rescue dog named Pickle, something in me lifted. With her one wonky eye, snaggle tooth, and sprinkling of gray hair, she appeared to be smiling at the camera, and I just knew she belonged with us. Sometimes you've got to think of your heart like a crowded park bench. Just politely ask the broken bits to skootch over and make a little space for happiness to sit down.

A LITTLE ACTION ON THE SIDE

VEGETABLES, ETC.

A good side dish is like a good partner in life: there to support you and balance you, humble you if necessary, and hang back when it's your time to shine. And on days when things go a little sideways, they step up and cover for you. Never so much the better half, but rather the other half, and the one that completes you and makes you whole. Bet you didn't know vegetables could be so romantic, did you?

I put the word *sprinkles* in this title and suddenly asparagus seems like a fun vegetable. I tried this on my tax returns, and my accountant still isn't talking to me.

Asparagus with Pancetta Sprinkles

Makes 4 to 6 servings

2 pounds asparagus

1 tablespoon olive oil

Salt and pepper

10 slices pancetta (about 5 ounces)

Zest of 1 lemon

¾ cup finely grated Parmesan

1 tablespoon finely chopped flat-leaf parsley

Preheat the oven to 400°F. Line a cookie sheet with parchment paper.

Remove the tough ends from the asparagus by lightly bending each stalk until it naturally snaps, leaving you with the tenderest part. Spread the asparagus on the prepared cookie sheet, drizzle with olive oil, and sprinkle with salt and pepper.

Bake for 15 to 20 minutes, making sure to give the pan a little shake at the halfway mark.

Meanwhile, in a nonstick skillet over medium heat, fry the pancetta slices in batches of three or four for about 2 minutes. Use metal tongs to turn the pancetta over and cook until they are a light golden brown and just starting to get crispy. Place the cooked pancetta on a plate lined with paper towel to absorb any excess fat. Repeat with the next batch.

Transfer the pancetta to a cutting board and use a large knife to chop it up. Some of the crispier bits will break up naturally. Place the pancetta bits in a medium bowl and add the lemon zest, grated Parmesan, and parsley. Stir to combine.

Remove the asparagus from the oven and arrange on a serving dish. Sprinkle the pancetta mix over the top and serve.

*M*y favorite way to cook pretty much any vegetable: roasted at high temp on a cookie sheet. These little guys are wonderful as a side with meatloaf, tucked inside a sandwich or omelet, or tossed with some pasta. So roast up a big tray and keep them in the refrigerator for the week. You won't be sorry.

Roasted Cherry Tomatoes

Makes 4 to 6 servings

4 cups (2 pints) cherry tomatoes

1 tablespoon olive oil

Generous sprinkle of sea salt and pepper

1 teaspoon dried Italian seasoning

Preheat the oven to 400°F. Line a cookie sheet with parchment paper.

Spread the tomatoes across the prepared cookie sheet. Drizzle with olive oil and sprinkle with the sea salt, pepper, and dried herbs. Give the pan a couple of shakes to roll the tomatoes around and coat them in the oil and seasoning.

Bake for 20 minutes, until the tomatoes start to soften and shrink.

Remove from the oven and serve hot. Alternatively, allow to cool and store, covered, in the refrigerator for up to 3 days.

*A*ll those times you found yourself wishing you could eat pizza with a spoon, I heard you.

Tomato Casserole

Makes 6 servings

2 tablespoons olive oil

4 pounds vine tomatoes, quartered, seeded, and cut in 2-inch chunks

1 medium onion, peeled and roughly chopped

6 cups bread cubes, crust left on (1-inch cubes) (see note)

1½ teaspoons salt

1 teaspoon pepper

2 cups grated sharp Cheddar

1 cup finely chopped basil

Preheat the oven to 350°F. Lightly butter a 9-inch round baking dish.

Heat the olive oil in a large skillet over medium heat. Add the chopped tomatoes and onions and cook until they begin to soften and break down, 5 to 7 minutes. Add the bread cubes, stir to combine, and continue to cook for several minutes, until the bread begins to soften as it absorbs the juices and oil. Add the salt and pepper.

Remove the pan from the heat and stir in the grated cheese and basil. Transfer to the prepared pan and use the back of a spoon or spatula to spread the top even. Bake for 30 minutes, until the top is browned and the tomatoes are bubbling.

PSSST . . . *I like to use a hearty bread for this dish rather than a simple French bread. Consider something that has whole wheat or rye flour in it, which will add a more interesting flavor to the overall dish.*

*I*f you went to high school with zucchini, you probably wouldn't have noticed it—until your 20-year grad reunion and it walks in wearing chili flakes and mint, and suddenly you feel a little stupid.

Roasted Zucchini with Chili Flakes and Mint

Makes 4 to 6 servings

2 pounds zucchini (about 4 medium)

2 tablespoons olive oil

Generous sprinkle of salt and pepper

1 tablespoon anise seeds

2 teaspoons chili flakes

1 tablespoon finely chopped mint

¼ cup sour cream

Preheat the oven to 425°F. Line a cookie sheet with parchment paper

Wash and dry the zucchini. Cut each zucchini into 1-inch pieces and spread across the prepared cookie sheet. Drizzle with the olive oil and sprinkle with the salt, pepper, anise seeds, and chili flakes.

Bake for 15 to 20 minutes, using a spatula to turn the zucchini pieces at the halfway point to ensure even browning, until the zucchini is brown and fragrant. Remove from the oven and transfer to a serving dish.

Sprinkle the fresh mint on top and gently toss. Give the sour cream a good stir to loosen it a little, then scoop it on top of the warm zucchini. Serve.

*P*aul Daykin gets full credit for this one. I'll be the first to say that I thought he was a little nuts (but then I usually am) when he suggested this combo, but one mouthful and I was convinced otherwise.

Green Beans with Cherry Tomatoes, Chorizo, and Goat Cheese

Makes 4 to 6 servings

1 pound green beans, ends trimmed

1½ cups chopped cured Spanish chorizo sausage (1-inch pieces)

1½ cups halved cherry tomatoes

½ teaspoon salt

½ cup crumbled goat cheese

Generous sprinkle of pepper

Fill a large pot with liberally salted water. Bring it to a boil, then add the green beans and cook for about 2 minutes. Drain and immediately place in a large bowl filled with ice water to stop the cooking process. Drain again and set aside.

In a large skillet over medium-high heat, cook the chorizo until it's starting to brown, about 5 minutes. Add the tomatoes and continue to cook for 1 to 2 minutes, until they begin to soften. Add the blanched beans and stir to combine. Season with salt.

Transfer the beans, chorizo, and tomatoes to a serving platter and sprinkle with the crumbled goat cheese. Pour over any pan juices and sprinkle with pepper. Serve immediately.

- 1 tablespoon butter
- 1 shallot, peeled and finely diced
- 1 pound mixed mushrooms (I chose shiitake, button, and cremini, but you can always switch it up with your favorites)
- 1 tablespoon finely chopped flat-leaf parsley
- 2 tablespoons sour cream

*T*his is definitely more of an on-top dish than a side dish. Perfect on top of a slice of meatloaf or a buttery piece of toast!

Fried Mushrooms with Sour Cream

Makes 4 to 6 servings

In a large skillet over medium heat, melt the butter and sauté the diced shallots until they're a lovely golden brown and just starting to caramelize, 5 to 7 minutes.

Wash the mushrooms and trim and discard the stems, then thickly slice the mushroom tops. Add the sliced mushrooms to the pan and continue to sauté until they have softened and browned, about 10 more minutes.

Add the chopped parsley and sour cream and continue to stir over the heat for another 2 minutes or so until everything has come together in a lovely creamy coating. Remove from the heat and serve.

*I*f this recipe ever shows up at your door asking for a job, you'd be a fool not to hire it! This is the hardest-working recipe out there.

Roasted Veg

Makes 4 to 6 servings

1 medium eggplant, peeled and cut in ½-inch cubes

1 red onion, peeled and cut in ½-inch slices

1 yellow pepper, seeded and cut in ½-inch pieces

1 red pepper, seeded and cut in ½-inch pieces

2 medium zucchini, halved and cut in ½-inch slices

¼ cup olive oil

2 teaspoons salt

1 teaspoon pepper

2 teaspoons dried Italian seasoning

Preheat the oven to 400°F. Line two cookie sheets with parchment paper.

Divide and spread the prepared vegetables evenly across the two cookie sheets. Drizzle each with olive oil, salt, pepper, and Italian seasoning. It's important to spread the vegetables across two pans to avoid overcrowding them, which would cause them to steam instead of roast and stop you from getting the nice charred crispy bits you're looking for.

Place both pans in the oven and roast for about 15 minutes. Rotate the pans, then use a spatula to toss and turn the vegetables to ensure even roasting. Continue to cook for about another 15 minutes, until all the vegetables have cooked through and are nicely browned.

Remove from the oven and serve hot. Alternatively, allow to cool and store, covered, in the refrigerator for up to 5 days.

This carrot dish is a little sweet and a little spicy. If it just wore glasses and had a lousy sense of direction, it could be me.

Honey Carrots with Spice and Yogurt

Makes 4 to 6 servings

3 pounds medium carrots

2 tablespoons olive oil

1 teaspoon ground cumin

1 teaspoon smoked paprika

½ teaspoon cayenne pepper

Generous sprinkle of sea salt and pepper

4 tablespoons honey

1 cup plain Greek yogurt

3 tablespoons finely chopped mint

Preheat the oven to 375°F. Line a cookie sheet with parchment paper.

Spread the carrots across the prepared cookie sheet and drizzle with olive oil. Sprinkle the spices, salt, and pepper evenly across the carrots, then drizzle with 2 tablespoons honey. Give the pan a little shake to roll the carrots and help coat them.

Bake for 25 to 30 minutes, giving the pan another shake at the halfway point to help the carrots brown evenly, until the carrots are browned all around.

Meanwhile, place the yogurt, the remaining 2 tablespoons honey, and the mint in a small bowl and stir to combine.

Remove the carrots from the oven and transfer to a serving platter. I like to serve them with a big dollop of the yogurt mixture on top for ease and presentation. Bring the balance of the yogurt to the table for anyone who wants a top-up.

This is an easy dish to make in the summer months with fresh corn or throughout the year with frozen. The crème fraîche adds a nice little tang, but if you don't have any on hand, you can always substitute with sour cream.

Corn Pudding

Makes 6 servings

½ cup all-purpose flour

½ cup cornmeal

1 tablespoon thyme leaves

1 teaspoon salt

½ teaspoon pepper

1 cup milk

1 cup crème fraîche

4 eggs, separated

2 tablespoons butter, melted

2 cups fresh corn kernels (if using frozen, thaw first)

1 cup grated smoked Gruyère (see note)

Preheat the oven to 350°F. Lightly butter a 9 × 13-inch casserole dish.

Place the flour, cornmeal, thyme, salt, and pepper in a large bowl and stir to combine.

In another bowl, whisk together the milk, crème fraîche, egg yolks, and melted butter. Add to the dry ingredients and stir to combine. Add the corn and mix again.

In a stand mixer fitted with the paddle attachment, whip the egg whites until stiff but not dry.

Gently fold the egg whites into the corn mixture, then fold in the grated cheese.

Spread the batter evenly into the prepared dish and bake for 15 to 20 minutes, until the top is browned and the center is only slightly loose.

PSSST . . . *I love the taste of the smoked Gruyère, but you can always substitute with a sharp Cheddar or regular Gruyère, or a combo of the two.*

hink of these potatoes like little Christmas presents. No peeking till it's time!

Don't Lift the Lid Potatoes

Makes 4 to 6 servings

¼ cup butter

2 cloves garlic, peeled and finely chopped

2 pounds baby red potatoes

1 teaspoon salt

½ teaspoon pepper

¼ cup finely chopped flat-leaf parsley

1 tablespoon finely chopped thyme leaves

In a large pot or Dutch oven over medium-high heat, melt the butter and sauté the garlic for about 2 minutes. Add the potatoes, salt, pepper, and half the parsley and thyme. Stir to combine and allow the potatoes to cook for about 2 minutes to ensure everything in the pot is nice and hot.

Put the lid on the pot and turn the temperature to low. Don't lift the lid for 40 to 45 minutes. You will want to give the pot a little shake every 10 minutes to ensure the potatoes brown evenly (but don't shake too hard or you'll be serving smashed potatoes and I'll have to change the name of the recipe).

Once the potatoes are fork-tender (meaning a fork will easily pierce the potato without breaking it apart), add the remaining parsley and thyme and stir to coat evenly. Season with a little more salt and pepper to your taste, and serve.

Store leftovers, covered, in the refrigerator for up to 3 days. You can reheat them in the microwave or slice and fry them up, with just a little butter, in a cast-iron skillet.

*T*he secret to a great mashed potato starts with the potato (Yukon Gold, please) and ends with the masher (if you don't own a potato ricer, stop reading this and go out and get one).

Fluffy Mashed Potatoes with Boursin Cheese

(actually, Boursin with a little mashed potato)

Makes 6 servings

3 pounds Yukon Gold potatoes

½ cup heavy cream

1 package Boursin cheese (it comes in a range of flavors, and shallot and chive is my fave)

2 tablespoons butter

2 teaspoons salt

Using a vegetable peeler or a small paring knife, peel the potatoes and cut them in quarters. Place them in a large pot filled with salted water over high heat and bring them to a boil. Reduce the heat and allow the potatoes to simmer until you can easily poke them with a fork, 15 to 20 minutes.

Drain the potatoes in a colander, then cover the colander with a clean tea towel for several minutes. The towel will absorb the excess moisture and steam.

While the potatoes are sitting, place the cream, Boursin cheese, and butter in a small saucepan and heat over medium heat until the cheese has melted and the cream is warm. Set aside.

Place your potato ricer over a large mixing bowl and proceed to process the cooked potatoes. The potato ricer is the perfect tool for getting all the lumps out while still keeping the potatoes light and fluffy. The more you stir or mash your potatoes, the gluier they become, so remember that a light hand is best.

Gently fold the warm cream and cheese mixture into the potatoes, then add the salt. Have a taste and salt a little more if you so desire. Transfer the finished potatoes to a serving dish and enjoy.

You can make the potatoes up to a day ahead. Store, covered, in the refrigerator and reheat in the microwave prior to serving.

I've always loved homemade baked beans, but they can be time consuming to make. Most recipes ask that you soak the beans in water overnight prior to baking them in the oven for 6 to 8 hours. That's quite a commitment for beans. I mean, I like them, but I don't want to marry them! So I decided to use the overnight part for baking instead of soaking. It worked like a charm and the kitchen smelled delicious all night long!

Maple Baked Beans

Makes 6 to 8 servings

1 pound dried navy beans

3 cups water, plus more for the initial boil

5 slices thick-cut bacon, chopped in 1-inch pieces

1 onion, peeled and finely chopped

½ cup pure maple syrup

2 tablespoons peeled and grated fresh ginger

2 tablespoons fancy molasses

2 tablespoons dark brown sugar

2 tablespoons Dijon mustard

2 tablespoons bourbon

1 teaspoon salt

½ teaspoon pepper

Preheat the oven to 225°F.

Place the beans in a large pot filled with water over high heat. Bring to a boil, then reduce heat and allow to simmer for 1 hour. Drain the beans and transfer them to a medium Dutch oven. Add the remaining ingredients to the beans and stir to combine. Place the lid on and bake in the preheated oven for about 12 hours.

Remove from the oven and serve hot. Store, covered, in the refrigerator for 3 to 4 days.

This is really two recipes in one, because to make risotto cakes, first you have to make risotto. Which is honestly just as delicious, but not something you can prepare in advance and keep, and I am all about anything that you can prepare in advance.

Risotto Cakes

Makes 6 cakes

5 cups chicken stock
  (page 99 or store-bought)

3 tablespoons butter

2 tablespoons olive oil

½ cup peeled and finely
  chopped onions

1½ cups arborio rice

½ cup white wine

½ teaspoon salt

½ teaspoon pepper

½ cup finely grated
  Parmesan

2 tablespoons finely chopped
  flat-leaf parsley

Zest of 1 lemon

Butter an 8-inch square baking pan and line with parchment paper. Set aside.

In a medium pot over high heat, bring the chicken stock to a boil. Remove from the heat and set aside.

In a large saucepan, melt 1 tablespoon butter and the olive oil over medium heat. Add the onions and sauté until translucent and soft. Add the rice and continue to sauté for several minutes until it too starts to appear slightly translucent. Add the wine, salt, and pepper and keep stirring until the wine has mostly cooked into the rice.

Add a ladleful of the hot chicken stock and keep stirring until most of the stock has been absorbed, making sure to reduce the heat to a simmer so the stock doesn't boil too quickly and cook only the outside of the rice. Add your next ladleful and repeat. Continue until all the stock has been absorbed. Have a taste and make sure the rice is cooked through. If you run out of stock before you feel the rice is done, you can add some boiling water. All in all, it should take you 15 to 20 minutes to cook the rice.

Remove the pan from the heat and gently stir in the Parmesan, parsley, lemon zest, and 1 tablespoon butter. Check your seasoning and add a little more salt and pepper if need be. At this point, you can abandon the plan for cakes and serve the risotto as is, or you can carry on to the next step.

Spread the risotto into the prepared pan and use the back of a spoon or small offset spatula to smooth flat. Chill the risotto in the refrigerator for at least 1 hour.

Remove the pan from the refrigerator and turn the risotto out onto a cutting board. Use a large knife to cut the risotto into six equal pieces. Melt the remaining 1 tablespoon butter in a nonstick skillet and fry the cakes for 4 to 6 minutes per side, until they are a lovely golden brown.

Store the risotto cakes, covered, in the refrigerator for up to 3 days.

CLEAN PLATE

I have a hard time working in a messy environment. I can't think at a desk covered in papers, I can't fall asleep in an unmade bed, and I can't cook with a sink full of dirty dishes. I'm sure I could still do all those things if I really had to, but I'd be in a lousy mood. Sometimes I wish I was a little more relaxed, but I guess it's just the way I'm wired. While I can handle a lot of chaos and stress in my daily life (in fact, my husband believes I'd have a hard time functioning without it), I learned a long time ago that a sense of order and place is a must in my physical world if I want a good night's rest.

When Paul and I first moved in together 30-plus years ago, we rented the main floor of an old house. Our suite had equal amounts of character and quirkiness, and we have nothing but fond memories of our time there—that is, of course, if you don't count the grumpy couple living upstairs who resented our constant entertaining, and the guy in the basement who held band practice every day. It was kind of like living through some weird form of immersion therapy to break us of a bad '80s rock habit.

I remember the night when I discovered that my desire for everything to be shipshape was stronger than the pull of sleep. Paul and I had hosted one of our first dinner parties, shortly after moving in together. We invited all our friends, set a rather mismatched table, turned up the music, and drank and ate ourselves silly. In those days, given how little we had, entertaining of any kind inevitably meant that every dish and glass would be used. Our rental came with an old-school dishwasher: a sink of hot water and some tea towels. You can't miss what you don't have, and for us it never seemed like a big deal.

It was very late when our friends departed for home, and as we blew out the last of the candles, Paul and I drunkenly promised each other that we would deal with the cleanup in the morning. I awoke several hours later feeling more than a little parched. Desperate for water, I went in search of a clean glass. Earlier, in my haste to pass out, I had somehow forgotten to put on a nightie, and I now found myself standing stark naked in the dining room, staring at a sea of dirty dishes. My brain went on autopilot, and the next thing I knew, I was up to my elbows in a sink full of bubbles, wearing nothing but a pair of yellow rubber gloves. I washed and dried every piece, put them back in the cupboard, straightened everything up, and swept the floors. As the sun began to rise, I climbed back into bed and fell asleep with a contented smile on my face, all while Paul lay blissfully unaware of my late-night efforts. When he awoke the next morning, a little hungover and a lot confused, he rubbed his eyes in bewilderment. "Rosie . . . we did have a dinner party last night, didn't we?"

I simply answered him with a quizzical stare, making the satisfaction and comfort I felt from my cleaning bonanza all the sweeter.

THE
SAUCY
BITS

CONDIMENTS, ETC.

I like to think of this as mayonnaise's fancy cousin. And I love the tang of the lemon tucked in a chicken sandwich or dolloped on an asparagus salad. This aioli also works as a wonderful dip for your raw veggies or crab cakes.

Lemon Aioli

Makes about 1 cup

2 cloves garlic, peeled

½ cup olive oil

¼ cup vegetable oil

1 egg yolk

2 tablespoons fresh lemon juice

1 tablespoon Dijon mustard

1 teaspoon salt

Zest of 1 lemon

Preheat the oven to 400°F.

Place the garlic cloves on a small piece of foil and drizzle them with about 1 teaspoon olive oil. Pinch the top of the foil together to create a little pouch and bake for about 30 minutes, until the garlic is very soft and starting to caramelize around the edges. Remove from the oven and transfer to a small bowl. Use the back of a spoon to mash the garlic smooth.

Place the egg yolk, lemon juice, mustard, roasted garlic, and salt in a food processor or blender (I prefer a food processor for this one) and pulse to combine. While the food processor is running, slowly add the remaining oil in a slow, thin, steady stream. Continue running the processor until all the oil has been incorporated and the aioli has thickened, 2 to 3 minutes. Fold in the lemon zest and transfer to a small bowl.

Cover with plastic wrap and refrigerate for at least 1 hour prior to use. Store, covered, in the refrigerator for 3 to 4 days.

½ cup ketchup

⅓ cup honey

⅓ cup dark brown sugar

3 tablespoons apple cider vinegar

2 tablespoons Dijon mustard

1 tablespoon peeled and grated fresh ginger

1 tablespoon Worcestershire sauce

2 teaspoons smoked paprika

1 teaspoon cayenne pepper

1 teaspoon salt

½ teaspoon pepper

*T*his is such an easy recipe made of ingredients that you no doubt have in your pantry, so I encourage you to give it a go. Don't hesitate to change it up to suit your taste if you want something a little spicier or sweeter.

Honey Barbecue Sauce

Makes about 1 cup

In a small saucepan over medium heat, whisk all of the ingredients together. Bring the sauce to a boil, reduce the heat, and allow to simmer for 15 minutes. Remove from the heat.

Store, covered, in the refrigerator for up to 1 month.

1 cup mayonnaise

2 tablespoons peeled and finely chopped shallots

2 tablespoons grainy mustard

1 tablespoon finely chopped flat-leaf parsley

1 teaspoon thyme leaves

1 teaspoon drained capers

3 dashes Tabasco

1 teaspoon salt

½ teaspoon pepper

*I*f mayonnaise had a wild side, this would be it! This condiment works well at livening up a ham sandwich or adding a little more depth to a classic tuna one.

Spicy Remoulade

Makes about 1 cup

Place all ingredients in a blender and blend on high for several minutes until well combined. Transfer to a small bowl, cover with plastic wrap, and chill in the refrigerator for at least 1 hour.

Store, covered, in the refrigerator for up to 2 weeks.

1 cup mayonnaise

¼ cup finely chopped gherkin pickles

2 teaspoons Dijon mustard

2 tablespoons finely chopped dill

1 tablespoon finely chopped tarragon

1 tablespoon drained capers

1 teaspoon Worcestershire sauce

1 teaspoon fresh lemon juice

½ teaspoon salt

Zest of 1 lemon

 little something for the fish in your life.

Tartar Sauce

Makes about 2 cups

Place all of the ingredients in a bowl and stir to combine. Cover and refrigerate for at least 30 minutes prior to serving. Store, covered, in the refrigerator for up to 1 week.

2 tablespoons butter

2 pounds sweet onions, peeled and finely chopped

About 2 cups water, room temperature

fter 24 years, India Daykin finally shared her recipe for making delicious caramelized onions with me. Kids can be so damn secretive.

India's Onion Jam

Makes about 2 cups

In a large cast-iron skillet over medium-high heat, melt the butter. Add the onions and cook until the pan starts to dry out and the onions begin to stick, about 10 minutes.

Add enough water to the pan to coat the bottom and remove any of the sticking onions. Continue to cook until the onions have caramelized (turning into a lovely dark brown, delicious, jammy mess), adding another bit of water every time the pan dries out. All in all, this will take you about 1 hour to complete. This sounds a little crazy, I know, but all good things come to those who wait.

Store, covered, in the refrigerator for 3 to 4 days or in the freezer for up to 3 months.

WALNUT PESTO

SPICY REMOULADE

INDIA'S ONION JAM

LEMON AIOLI

TARTAR SAUCE

SMOKY TOMATO RELISH

HOMEMADE BUTTER

I love this relish inside a fried-egg sandwich, but it's equally good with a grilled cheese or meatloaf sandwich.

Smoky Tomato Relish

Makes about 2 cups

1 tablespoon olive oil

2 pounds Roma tomatoes, seeded and finely chopped

½ cup peeled and finely chopped onions

½ cup finely chopped sun-dried tomatoes

2 tablespoons dark brown sugar

1 tablespoon apple cider vinegar

1 teaspoon salt

1 teaspoon smoked paprika

½ teaspoon celery seeds

½ teaspoon dried mustard

¼ cup water

Place the olive oil, Roma tomatoes, and onions in a large skillet over medium-high heat. Cook until the tomatoes and onions are very soft and broken down, about 15 minutes.

Add the remaining ingredients and cook until the relish has thickened slightly, about 10 minutes. Remove from the heat and transfer to a bowl.

Store, covered, in the refrigerator for up to 1 week.

*M*ost pesto is made with pine nuts, which are delicious but also pretty spendy. I prefer to use walnuts, which are a little more cost effective and impart a nuttier flavor. Spread this pesto in veggie sandwiches, toss your pasta in it, or swap out your usual pizza sauce with it.

Walnut Pesto

Makes about 1 cup

2 cloves garlic, peeled

2/3 cup plus 1 teaspoon olive oil

1/2 cup walnut pieces

3 cups basil leaves

1/2 cup grated Parmesan

1 teaspoon salt

1 teaspoon fresh lemon juice

PSSST . . . *To turn this into Mint Pesto, simply swap out the basil leaves with 3 cups of mint leaves.*

Preheat the oven to 400°F.

Place the garlic cloves on a small piece of foil and drizzle them with 1 teaspoon olive oil. Pinch the top of the foil together to create a little pouch and bake for about 30 minutes, until the garlic is very soft and starting to caramelize around the edges. Remove from the oven and set aside to cool.

Reduce the oven temperature to 350°F. Line a cookie sheet with parchment paper.

Spread the walnuts across the prepared cookie sheet and roast in the oven for 10 to 15 minutes, until golden brown and fragrant. Remove from the oven and set aside to cool.

In a food processor or blender, combine the roasted garlic and walnuts with the remaining ingredients. Pulse to combine until smooth, about 1 minute.

Store, covered, in the refrigerator for 1 week or in the freezer for up to 3 months.

I've learned that all you need to make butter is some heavy cream, a food processor, and some cheesecloth. Which is really fortunate, because the damn cow wouldn't fit in my appliance cupboard.

Homemade Butter

Makes 1 pound of butter

4 cups heavy cream

About 1 cup ice water

1 to 2 teaspoons sea salt
   (optional)

Pour the cream into a 12-cup food processor. Turn it on and run until the cream solids start to separate and form into butter, about 5 minutes (you can use a stand mixer for this too, but make sure you're working on low speed or the cream will start flying around the kitchen).

Pour off any buttermilk that has formed. This is a very important step, as excess buttermilk will cause your butter to go rancid much quicker. You can save the buttermilk and cook with it or drink it up.

Take a piece of cheesecloth and fold it over several times. Remove the butter from the food processor and wrap it in the cheesecloth. Give it a little squeeze to remove any remaining buttermilk. Unfold the butter from the cheesecloth and place it back in the food processor.

Pour a couple of tablespoons of ice water down the shoot of the food processor and pulse several times. Remove the lid and pour off the water. Continue to repeat this step until the water is no longer cloudy.

If you are making salted butter, you can now add the salt and pulse to combine. Transfer the finished butter to a small bowl.

Store, covered, in the refrigerator for up to 1 week. If you aren't planning on putting butter on everything you make all week long, you can always freeze some of it, tightly wrapped, for up to 6 months.

I created this butter to work with my Roasted Chicken recipe (page 164), but it would be just as delicious on top of a piece of salmon or a tenderloin steak.

Dijon Herb Butter

About 1 cup

¼ cup thyme leaves

¼ cup finely chopped rosemary

¼ cup finely chopped sage leaves

1 tablespoon lemon zest

1 cup butter, room temperature

2 tablespoons grainy Dijon mustard

Place all the ingredients in a stand mixer fitted with the paddle attachment and beat on high until well combined.

Place a piece of plastic wrap on the kitchen counter, then transfer the butter mixture on top of the wrap. Shape the butter into a log about 6 inches long × 2 inches across, then wrap tightly in the plastic wrap. Place the log in the refrigerator and allow it to chill until firm, 25 to 30 minutes, before slicing.

Store in the refrigerator for up to 1 week or well wrapped in the freezer for up to 3 months.

SPONTANEOUS
MOMENTS

I'm a planner. This trait, combined with being a morning person, definitely puts me in the running for most annoying human ever. I like to begin my days by greeting Paul with a cheery, "What's the plan, Stan?" I don't mean to get on his nerves, but I'm a firm believer that a little structure goes a long way to making a happy life—or at the very least, a somewhat productive day.

But every now and again, I'm reminded that sometimes having no plans can ultimately be the best plan and that spontaneous moments, whether good or bad, always leave the greatest impression.

In my previous working life as an interior designer, Paul and I spent much of our early years together buying, renovating, and selling homes. I'm not sure how I continually managed to convince him that this was a good idea, but I love him all the more for it. We have lived in a total of nine homes over the last 30 years, each unique and equally loved. But number six holds a really special place in our hearts, because that's where we were lucky enough to meet the Murphys.

Cam and Margie Murphy and their girls, Claire and Elizabeth, lived only two doors up the street, and once we were introduced, it didn't take long for us to consider them family. There is something truly magical about life when you can call your neighbors friends. Sharing a meal is as simple as a knock on the door. No need to coordinate your schedules and book a date, you're already practically home. Suddenly a casual dinner on a weeknight is possible. No fanfare, no floral arrangements, no complicated appetizers—just some conversation and laughs before everyone heads home to bed. Life just feels richer when you're able to share the everyday stuff.

I'll never forget the New Year's Eve we turned up on the Murphys' doorstep long before the stroke of midnight. We had been for dinner with my parents, and given India's young age, planned to go to bed early and welcome the new year over breakfast the next morning. But the Murphys were having none of that. Without hesitation, they insisted we stay and join them in their annual tradition of a lobster feast around the coffee table. We soon discovered that the secret to being able to indulge in a second dinner is washing it down with lots of champagne and laughter.

The kids stayed up way past bedtime so we could all bang pots and pans on the front porch when the clock struck 12. It was a perfect night made all the more so by our hosts' spontaneity and kindness. It was made even more memorable for me when I woke the next morning to discover my face covered in a strange rash. How could this be? Could I have developed an allergy to lobster . . . or worse yet, champagne? I knew my body would never betray me and revolt against champagne, but apparently it does get a little testy when I mistakenly apply peppermint foot cream to my face in lieu of my nightly moisturizer. Some things you just can't plan.

FOR YOUR DESSERT COMPART-MENT

DESSERT

When India was a wee little girl, she loved dinner as long as it was pasta with cheese, bread with cheese, or cheese pizza. This worked out great about 10 percent of the time. I'm sure I'm not the only parent who has struggled in vain to get their child to finish their chicken and broccoli only to be met with a confident, "I'm full, Mama."

The first time I heard this, I wasn't too concerned. I thought I knew how to deal with it. I calmly explained that if she was too full for dinner, then, sadly, she mustn't have any room for dessert either. Her three-year-old self turned to me, with eyes full of pity for my clear lack of understanding of human anatomy, and said, "Silly Mama, only my dinner compartment is full. My dessert compartment is empty!"

*T*here is something about sprinkles that just sets the world on fire. Okay, maybe not the whole world, but definitely Instagram.

If Friday Were a Cake

Makes 1 (8-inch) layer cake, 8 to 12 servings

2¾ cups pastry flour

1 tablespoon baking powder

½ teaspoon salt

1½ cups buttermilk, room temperature

2 teaspoons pure vanilla

¾ cup butter, room temperature

1¾ cups granulated sugar

5 egg whites, room temperature

¼ cup rainbow sprinkles

1 recipe Pink Vanilla Butter Cream (see below)

Position the rack in the center of the oven and preheat to 350°F. Butter two 8-inch cake pans and line with parchment paper. Set aside.

On a large piece of parchment, sift the flour, baking powder, and salt. Set aside.

Combine the buttermilk and vanilla in a bowl and set aside.

In a stand mixer fitted with the paddle attachment, beat the butter and sugar on medium-high until pale and fluffy. Scrape down the sides of the bowl. Turn the mixer to low and add the egg whites, then increase speed to high and beat until thick and smooth. Scrape down the sides of the bowl.

With the mixer running on low, add the dry ingredients in three parts, alternating with the buttermilk mixture, beginning and ending with the dry. Scrape down the sides of the bowl. Gently fold in the rainbow sprinkles.

Divide the batter evenly between the two prepared pans and smooth the tops flat with a rubber spatula. Give the pans a couple of light taps on the counter to deflate any overly large air pockets.

Bake on the center rack for 30 to 40 minutes, until the tops are a pale golden color and spring back a little when pressed lightly with your fingertip. Remove from the oven and allow the cakes to cool in the pans for about 10 minutes before inverting them onto wire racks to cool completely.

When the cakes are cool, use a large serrated knife to cut each one in half horizontally, making sure to keep the blade level as you cut, to create four layers in total. If that seems daunting, you can always leave the cakes as they are and make a two-layer cake.

Nearly done

Place the bottom layer of cake on a cake board or large plate. Using an offset spatula, spread about ½ cup of the pink vanilla butter cream evenly over the cake layer. Top with the next layer and repeat until you have placed the last layer on top.

With the back of the offset spatula, smooth a thin layer of butter cream across the top and down the sides of the cake. Rotate your spatula back and forth to evenly and thoroughly coat the cake with butter cream, making sure to remove any excess. This thin layer of butter cream will act as your crumb coat, locking down any crumbs. Place the cake in the refrigerator for about 15 minutes to allow the crumb coat to set up.

Remove the cake from the refrigerator and place a large dollop of butter cream on top. Use your offset spatula to smooth the icing across the top and down the sides of the cake. Apply more icing to the sides of the cake and smooth it out with your spatula. This will cause the butter cream to build up around the top edge of the cake. Use the spatula to drag the edge of butter cream across the top of the cake, which will help create a sharp straight edge rather than a rounded one.

If you have some sprinkles left over, you can sprinkle them around the top of the cake to give people a hint of what is to come inside. Now, cut a slice and enjoy your weekend!

Store before icing, covered, for up to 3 days, or frozen for up to 1 month.

Pink Vanilla Butter Cream

Makes about 5 cups, enough for 1 (8-inch, 4-layer) cake

2 cups butter, room temperature

4 cups icing sugar, sifted

⅓ cup whole milk

2 tablespoons pure vanilla

6 to 8 drops red food coloring (see note)

In a stand mixer fitted with the paddle attachment, beat the butter on high speed until very fluffy and pale yellow. Turn the mixer to low and add the icing sugar. Continue to beat on low until well combined. Scrape down the sides of the bowl.

Add the milk, vanilla, and food coloring and beat again on low to combine. Turn the mixer to high and continue to beat until the icing is light and fluffy, about 10 minutes.

PSSST . . . *It's only pink because I made it so. You can choose to switch up the color or skip this step entirely. I prefer to use natural food coloring, which I've found at Whole Foods or online through India Tree.*

I'm a big fan of grapefruit and of cupcakes, so for me this recipe just makes sense. If you aren't a fan of grapefruit, swap it out for lemon or orange. If you aren't a fan of cupcakes, what's wrong with you?

Pink Grapefruit Cupcakes

Makes 12 cupcakes

1 cup self-rising flour

1 cup all-purpose flour

½ teaspoon salt

½ cup butter, room temperature

1¼ cups granulated sugar

2 eggs

⅔ cup milk

⅓ cup grapefruit juice

2 teaspoons pure vanilla

3 tablespoons grapefruit zest

2 drops red food coloring (optional)

1 recipe Pink Grapefruit Butter Cream (see below)

Preheat the oven to 350°F.

Sift together both flours and salt onto a large piece of parchment paper. Set aside.

In a stand mixer fitted with the paddle attachment, cream the butter and sugar on medium-high speed until light and fluffy. Scrape down the sides of the bowl. Add the eggs one at a time and beat well after each addition. Scrape down the sides of the bowl several times.

In a liquid measuring cup, whisk together the milk, grapefruit juice, and vanilla to combine.

Turn the mixer to low and add the dry ingredients in three parts, alternating with the milk mixture in two parts (begin and end with the dry). Scrape down the sides of the bowl several times to make sure everything is fully combined. Add 1 tablespoon grapefruit zest and the food coloring (if using) and mix again.

Line a 12-cup muffin pan with paper liners. Use an ice-cream scoop to fill each paper liner about three-quarters full with cake batter. Bake for 20 to 25 minutes or until a wooden skewer inserted in the center of a cupcake comes out clean. Remove the cupcakes from the oven and allow to cool in the pan for 10 minutes, then transfer to a wire rack to cool completely.

Fill a piping bag fitted with a large star tip with the butter cream. Hold the piping bag at a sharp angle above the cupcake. Start at the

This one's a real page turner

outer edge and slowly and carefully pipe your way around in a circle to the center of the cupcake. When you reach the center, stop piping and pull up quickly to create a little peak of icing. Repeat with remaining cupcakes. Sprinkle the top of each cupcake with some of the remaining grapefruit zest.

Store, covered, for up to 3 days, or in the freezer for up to 3 months.

Pink Grapefruit Butter Cream

Makes about 2 cups, enough for 12 cupcakes

1 cup butter, room temperature

3½ cups icing sugar

2 tablespoons grapefruit juice

1 tablespoon grapefruit zest

1 to 2 drops red food coloring (optional)

In a stand mixer fitted with the paddle attachment, beat the butter on high speed until very pale in color. Stop the mixer and scrape down the sides of the bowl at least twice while beating the butter.

Turn the mixer to low and slowly add the icing sugar. Mix until well combined, then slowly add the grapefruit juice. Scrape down the sides of the bowl. Add the grapefruit zest and food coloring (if using). Return the mixer to high speed and beat until the butter cream is light and fluffy, about 5 minutes.

PSSST . . . *You can always replace the grapefruit juice and zest with equivalent amounts of orange or lemon. If you're using a little food coloring to tint your butter cream, make sure to switch it up depending on the citrus you've chosen so as not to confuse the end user.*

*W*hen someone asks me how I take my tea, I always say by the slice with lots of glaze on top.

Lemon Earl Grey Pound Cake

Makes 1 (8-inch) loaf, 8 to 10 servings

Cake

1¾ cups all-purpose flour

¼ teaspoon salt

¼ cup buttermilk

1 teaspoon pure vanilla

2 tablespoons Earl Grey tea leaves

1 cup butter, room temperature

1⅓ cups granulated sugar

3 eggs, room temperature

Zest of 1 lemon

Glaze

½ cup granulated sugar

¼ cup fresh lemon juice

¼ cup butter

Preheat the oven to 350°F. Butter and flour an 8-inch loaf pan. Set aside.

Make the cake: Sift the flour and salt onto a piece of parchment paper and set aside. Place the buttermilk and vanilla in a bowl and set aside. Place the tea leaves in a blender and grind on high to create a powder. Set aside.

In a stand mixer fitted with the paddle attachment, cream the butter and sugar on high until light and fluffy. Scrape down the sides of the bowl. Turn the mixer to medium speed and add the eggs one at a time, beating well after each addition. Scrape down the sides of the bowl. With the mixer running on low, add the flour mixture and buttermilk mixture alternately, beginning and ending with the flour. Scrape down the sides of the bowl. Add the ground tea and lemon zest and beat again to combine.

Place the batter in the prepared pan and bake for 45 to 50 minutes or until a wooden skewer inserted in the center comes out clean. Remove from the oven and allow it to cool for about 10 minutes before removing from the pan and transferring to a wire rack to cool completely.

Make the glaze: In a small saucepan over medium heat, combine the sugar, lemon juice, and butter. Bring to a boil, then remove from the heat and set aside.

Once the loaf has cooled, gently spoon the glaze down the center, allowing the excess to run over the edge and down the sides (you may want to place a piece of parchment paper underneath to catch any drips).

Store, covered, for up to 1 week, or in the freezer for up to 3 months.

a showstopper of a dessert for the summer season! If you're feeling a little more restrained, you can always halve the recipe and make a single layer cake (every party needs a pooper).

Chocolate Berry Shortcake

Makes 1 (9-inch) layer cake, 8 servings

1 cup pastry flour

¼ cup dark cocoa

8 eggs, separated

1½ teaspoons cream of tartar

1¾ cups granulated sugar

1 teaspoon pure vanilla

Whipped Cream (page 266)

3 cups mixed fresh berries (strawberries, blueberries, blackberries, raspberries)

The Best Chocolate Sauce (page 267)

Preheat the oven to 350°F. Line two 9-inch circular cake pans with parchment paper and set aside.

Sift the flour and cocoa onto a piece of parchment paper and set aside.

Place the egg whites in the bowl of a stand mixer fitted with the whisk attachment and beat on high until foamy. Add the cream of tartar and beat on medium until soft peaks form. With the mixer still running, gradually add ¼ cup sugar and continue beating until stiff glossy peaks form. Transfer the egg whites to a large mixing bowl.

Return the bowl of the mixer to the stand, still fitted with the whisk attachment. Add the egg yolks, the remaining 1½ cups sugar, and the vanilla. Beat on high speed until the yolks are very pale yellow and have doubled in volume, 3 to 5 minutes. Gently fold the egg yolks into the stiff egg whites, then fold in the flour and cocoa.

Divide the batter evenly between the prepared cake pans and use a small offset spatula to spread it evenly across. Bake for 13 to 15 minutes, until the cake springs back when lightly touched.

Remove from the oven. Allow the cakes to cool in the pans for about 15 minutes before turning them out onto a wire rack to cool completely.

Turn the cakes top side up and place one on a serving plate. Spread a generous scoop of whipped cream across the cake and sprinkle with half of the mixed berries. Top with the remaining cake and repeat. Refrigerate until ready to serve.

Before serving, gently warm the chocolate sauce in a pan over low heat or for about a minute in the microwave (be careful not to overheat it—you want it just warm, not so hot it melts the whipped cream). Drizzle the sauce over the top of the cake and allow it to drip down the sides.

Store in the refrigerator for up to 3 days.

I love the simplicity of this one-layer cake, perfect for when you're in need of dessert but pressed for time. It comes together in a flash with no frosting required—just a little sprinkle of icing sugar and maybe a scoop of whipped cream.

Almond Blueberry Cake

Makes 1 (9-inch cake), about 8 servings

1½ cups all-purpose flour

2 teaspoons baking powder

½ teaspoon baking soda

½ teaspoon salt

¾ cup almond meal (ground almonds)

¾ cup butter, room temperature

1 cup granulated sugar

2 eggs

1 cup plain yogurt

1 teaspoon pure vanilla

1 tablespoon orange zest

1 cup fresh blueberries

Sprinkle of icing sugar (optional, for serving)

Whipped Cream (page 266) (optional, for serving)

Preheat the oven to 350°F. Butter and flour a 9-inch circular cake pan. Set aside.

Sift the flour, baking powder, baking soda, and salt onto a large piece of parchment paper. Add the almond meal and set aside.

In a stand mixer fitted with the paddle attachment, cream the butter and sugar on high speed until light and fluffy. Scrape down the sides of the bowl. Add the eggs one at a time, mixing well after each addition. Scrape down the sides of the bowl. Add the yogurt and vanilla and mix again. Turn the mixer to low and slowly add the dry ingredients until just combined. Remove the bowl from the stand and scrape down the sides. Gently fold in the orange zest and blueberries.

Spread the mixture evenly into the prepared cake pan. Bake for 35 to 40 minutes or until a wooden skewer inserted in the center comes out clean. Remove from the oven and allow to cool for 10 minutes before turning the cake out onto a wire rack to cool completely.

Invert the cake so the top is facing up and place it on a serving plate. Use a small sieve to lightly dust the top of the cake with icing sugar. Serve each slice with a dollop of whipped cream, if using.

Store, covered, for up to 1 week, or in the freezer for up to 3 months.

his cake should be admired for its understated elegance and subtle confidence, without relying on exotic flavors to make its point. I'm not sure if I should eat it or take fashion advice from it.

Crème Fraîche Bundt Cake

Makes 1 cake, 8 to 10 servings

3 cups pastry flour

1 teaspoon baking powder

½ teaspoon baking soda

½ teaspoon salt

1 cup butter, room temperature

1 cup granulated sugar

5 eggs

1 cup crème fraîche

1 teaspoon pure vanilla

1 tablespoon icing sugar, for sprinkling

Preheat the oven to 350°F. Butter and flour an 8-cup Bundt pan (see note) and set aside.

Sift the flour, baking powder, baking soda, and salt onto a large piece of parchment paper and set aside.

In a stand mixer fitted with the paddle attachment, cream the butter and sugar on high until light and fluffy. Scrape down the sides of the bowl.

In a medium bowl, whisk together the eggs, crème fraîche, and vanilla.

With the mixer running on low, add the dry ingredients in three parts, alternating with the crème fraîche mixture in two parts (begin and end with the dry). Scrape down the sides of the bowl after each addition.

Transfer the batter to the prepared Bundt pan and use a spatula to spread it evenly across the top. Bake for 45 to 50 minutes or until a wooden skewer inserted into the center of the cake comes out clean. Remove from the oven and allow to cool slightly in the pan before turning it out and transferring to a wire rack to cool completely. Once cool, use a small sieve to sprinkle the top of the cake with the icing sugar.

Store covered or in an airtight container in the fridge for up to 1 week, or in the freezer for up to 3 months.

PSSST . . . *Sizing a Bundt pan can be a little confusing, as they're generally measured in cups rather than inches. You can establish the capacity of your Bundt pan by filling it to the brim with water and then measuring the amount.*

On those days when your world turns upside down, it's nice to have an appropriate food supply.

Rhubarb Upside-Down Cake

Makes 1 (9-inch) cake, about 8 servings

2 cups all-purpose flour

2 teaspoons baking powder

1 teaspoon ground cinnamon

1½ teaspoons salt

1 cup butter, room
    temperature

1¾ cups granulated sugar

½ cup dark brown sugar

4 cups chopped fresh
    rhubarb (½-inch pieces)

2 eggs

1 cup buttermilk

1 teaspoon pure vanilla

Whipped Cream (page 266),
    for serving

PSSST... *You can change up the rhubarb with any fruit that's in season. I've used blueberries and plums before to great success!*

Preheat the oven to 350°F. Butter a 9-inch circular cake pan and line with parchment paper. Set aside.

Sift the flour, baking powder, cinnamon, and ½ teaspoon salt onto a large piece of parchment paper and set aside.

Place ¼ cup butter, ¾ cup granulated sugar, the brown sugar, and the remaining salt in a small bowl. Use a spoon to combine until a smooth paste forms. Spread the paste across the bottom of the prepared pan, then top with the chopped rhubarb pieces. Set aside.

In a stand mixer fitted with the paddle attachment, cream the remaining butter and sugar on high speed until light and fluffy. Scrape down the sides of the bowl. Add the eggs one at a time, making sure to beat well after each addition. Scrape down the sides of the bowl.

In a small liquid measuring cup, combine the buttermilk and vanilla. With the mixer running on low speed, add the dry ingredients in three parts, alternating with the buttermilk mixture in two parts, beginning and ending with the dry. Scape down the sides of the bowl several times during this process to make sure everything is properly combined.

Use a small offset spatula or the back of a spoon to spread the batter evenly into the pan over the rhubarb layer.

Bake for 40 to 45 minutes or until a wooden skewer inserted in the center comes out clean. Remove from the oven and allow it to cool for at least 10 minutes before turning it out onto a wire rack to cool completely.

Should you wish to serve the cake warm (which I strongly suggest!), just turn it straight out onto a cake dish and serve each slice with a dollop of whipped cream. One bite and I promise your world will be right side up again!

Store covered for up to 3 days or in the freezer for up to 3 months.

his is a delicious little something to have with a cup of tea at pretty much any time of day. If you find your pantry bare of pistachios, you can always replace them with ground almonds or hazelnuts.

Pistachio Raspberry Loaf

Makes 1 (8-inch) loaf, about 8 servings

Loaf

1¼ cups all-purpose flour

1½ teaspoons baking powder

1½ teaspoons salt

¾ cup unsalted shelled pistachios

1 cup butter, room temperature

1¼ cups granulated sugar

1½ teaspoons pure vanilla

3 eggs

¾ cup fresh (or frozen and thawed) raspberries

Glaze

1 cup icing sugar

2 tablespoons heavy cream

4 to 5 fresh raspberries

Preheat the oven to 350°F. Butter and flour an 8-inch loaf pan and set aside.

Make the loaf: Sift the flour, baking powder, and salt onto a large piece of parchment paper and set aside.

In a blender or food processor, grind the pistachios until fine. Set aside.

In a stand mixer fitted with the paddle attachment, cream the butter and sugar on medium-high speed until light and fluffy. Scrape down the sides of the bowl. Add the eggs one at a time and beat well after each addition. Scrape down the sides of the bowl. Add the vanilla and beat again to combine. Turn the mixer to low, slowly add the dry ingredients, and mix until just combined. Remove the bowl from the stand and gently fold in the ground pistachios and raspberries.

Spoon the batter into the prepared pan and use a spatula to smooth the top evenly.

Bake for 45 to 50 minutes or until a wooden skewer inserted in the center comes out clean. Remove from the oven and allow to cool slightly, then transfer to a wire rack to cool completely before glazing.

Make the glaze: In a small bowl, whisk together the icing sugar, cream, and raspberries to create a smooth glaze. Don't worry about the seeds, as I think they make a lovely little finishing detail.

Place a piece of parchment under the wire rack where the loaf has cooled. Slowly drizzle the glaze over the top of the loaf and let it drip down the sides. Allow to set for about 10 minutes before slicing.

Store covered for up to 1 week, or in the freezer for up to 3 months.

This recipe was created for Paul Custard Daykin. Actually his middle name is Murray, but in fairness to his mum, at the time he was born she had no idea how passionate he would grow to be about all things made with eggs and cream.

Rice Pudding with Raisins for Poolie

Makes 6 servings

⅔ cup raisins

⅓ cup rum

1 cup arborio rice

2 cups water

1 teaspoon salt

1½ cups milk

½ cup heavy cream

½ cup granulated sugar

2 egg yolks

1 tablespoon pure vanilla

2 teaspoons orange zest

Whipped Cream (page 266) (optional, for serving)

Orange peel (optional, for serving)

In a small bowl, combine the raisins and rum. Allow to sit for at least 1 hour so the raisins can soften and soak up all the rum.

In a small saucepan over high heat, combine the arborio rice, water, and salt. Bring the rice to a boil. Reduce the heat and simmer, covered, for about 20 minutes, undisturbed. Lift the lid and gently toss the rice with a fork. Fold a clean tea towel in half, drape it over the pot, and recover with the lid. Allow the rice to steam for 10 minutes with the towel in place. Remove the lid and set aside.

In a large saucepan over high heat, whisk together the milk, cream, sugar, egg yolks, vanilla, and orange zest. Add the rice and stir to combine. Cook over high heat until the mixture begins to boil. Reduce the heat to a simmer, cover, and continue to cook until thickened, about 15 minutes. Make sure to lift the lid and give it a stir every 5 minutes or so.

Remove from the heat and stir in the rum and raisins. Transfer to a serving bowl, cover with plastic wrap, and place in the refrigerator for at least 1 hour, until cool.

Paul will eat rice pudding just as it comes, but he is extra-happy when it's served with a dollop of whipped cream.

Store, covered, in the refrigerator for up to 3 days.

*T*rust me, I've met a few of them.

Nut Bars

Makes 16 bars

Base

½ cup butter, room
    temperature

1 cup dark brown sugar

1 teaspoon pure vanilla

2 eggs

1½ cups all-purpose flour

1 teaspoon salt

Topping

2 egg whites

¾ cup granulated sugar

2 tablespoons corn syrup

1½ cups unsalted mixed
    nuts (walnuts, almonds,
    hazelnuts, cashews)

Preheat the oven to 350°F. Butter a 9-inch square pan and line with parchment paper, letting two sides hang over the edge to create parchment "handles." Set aside.

Make the base: In a stand mixer fitted with the paddle attachment, cream the butter and sugar on medium-high until light and fluffy. Scrape down the sides of the bowl and add the vanilla. Add the eggs one at a time, making sure to mix well after each addition. Scrape down the sides of the bowl. Turn the mixer to low, add the flour and salt, and beat until well combined.

Spread the mixture into the prepared pan and use a small offset spatula or the back of a spoon to smooth it evenly across. Set aside.

Make the topping: Switch the paddle attachment for the whisk attachment and thoroughly wash and dry the mixer bowl to ensure there are no traces of fat left. Add the egg whites and beat on high speed until soft peaks form. Turn the mixer down to medium and slowly add the sugar and corn syrup and continue to beat until the meringue is shiny and holds stiff peaks, about 5 minutes. You can test this by turning off the mixer, sticking your spatula into the egg whites, and quickly pulling it out. When you hold the spatula upright, the meringue should hold a stiff peak.

Remove the bowl from the stand and gently fold in the mixed nuts. Spread the nut mixture evenly across the base. Bake in the preheated oven for 25 to 30 minutes, until the meringue top is a lovely golden brown. Remove from the oven and allow to cool completely in the pan.

Run a small knife along the two edges of the pan that do not have parchment handles. Carefully remove the slab from the pan and cut into about 2-inch square bars. Make sure to use at least a 10-inch knife to avoid cutting and dragging the knife across the bars.

Store in an airtight container for up to 1 week or in the freezer for up to 3 months.

ay back when, these were known as Millionaire Bars, but when I set out to make them, I figured I should factor something in for inflation.

Bajillionaire Bars

Makes 16 bars

Base

½ cup butter, room temperature

⅓ cup dark brown sugar

1½ cups all-purpose flour

Filling

1 cup butter

¾ cup granulated sugar

1 cup sweetened condensed milk

2 tablespoons corn syrup

Topping

1 cup semisweet chocolate chips

2 tablespoons butter

1 teaspoon sea salt flakes (I like Maldon)

Preheat the oven to 350°F. Butter a 9-inch square pan and line with parchment paper, letting two sides hang over the edge to create parchment "handles." Set aside.

Make the base: In a stand mixer fitted with the paddle attachment, cream the butter and sugar on medium speed until light and fluffy. Scrape down the sides of the bowl. Turn the mixer to low and add the flour. Continue to mix on low until well combined and the mixture appears sandy.

Firmly and evenly press the dough into the prepared pan. Bake for 10 to 12 minutes, until light golden brown around the edges. Remove from the oven and set aside.

Make the filling: In a medium saucepan over medium-low heat, melt the butter, sugar, condensed milk, and corn syrup. Attach a candy thermometer to the side of the pan. Cook the caramel, stirring constantly, until it has thickened and is a pale amber color and the candy thermometer reads 220°F. This should take about 10 minutes and you should adjust the heat as needed. Remove from the heat and carefully pour the caramel over the base layer, using a small offset spatula or the back of a spoon to smooth it out. Allow the caramel to set for about 20 minutes.

Make the topping: In a double boiler or in a heatproof bowl set over a saucepan of simmering water, melt the chocolate chips and butter. Pour over the caramel layer and spread evenly using a small offset spatula or the back of a spoon. Tap the pan on the countertop to help smooth the chocolate layer. Sprinkle the chocolate with sea salt flakes. Place the pan in the refrigerator for at least 1 hour, until the chocolate top has set.

Run a small knife along the two edges of the pan that do not have parchment handles. Carefully remove the slab from the pan and cut into about 2-inch square bars. Make sure to use at least a 10-inch knife to do this to avoid cutting and dragging the knife across the bars.

Store, covered, for up to 1 week or in the freezer for up to 3 months.

*Y*ou know the cookie is going to be good when the ingredients are so famous, they get their own celebrity mash-up name.

Nutnana Cookies

Makes 12 cookies

2 cups all-purpose flour

½ cup granulated sugar plus 2 tablespoons

¼ cup dark brown sugar

½ teaspoon baking soda

½ teaspoon salt

½ cup butter, room temperature

½ cup peanut butter

½ cup mashed banana (about 1 medium banana)

1 teaspoon pure vanilla

2 tablespoons peanut butter, for filling

In a stand mixer fitted with the paddle attachment, combine the flour, ½ cup of granulated sugar, the dark brown sugar, baking soda, and salt and beat once to combine. Add the butter and peanut butter and beat on medium speed for several minutes, until the mixture is crumbly. Add the banana and vanilla and continue to beat until the dough pulls together.

Remove the dough from the bowl, gently shape into a 12-inch-long log, and wrap tightly in plastic wrap. Allow to chill in the refrigerator for at least 1 hour, until the dough is firm to the touch.

Preheat the oven to 350°F. Line a cookie sheet with parchment paper and set aside.

Remove the dough from the refrigerator, unwrap, and use a large sharp knife to cut it into 24 equal slices. Place 12 of the slices, evenly spaced, on the prepared cookie sheet. Using two small teaspoons, place ½ teaspoon of peanut butter in the center of each slice of dough and top with the remaining slices. Place 2 tablespoons of sugar in a small bowl. Use a fork to seal the edges of each cookie, dipping the fork in the sugar as you go to prevent the times from sticking to the dough.

Place the cookies on the center rack of the oven and bake for 10 to 12 minutes, until they are a light golden brown around the edges. Remove from the oven and allow to cool slightly before transferring them to a wire rack to cool completely.

Store covered or in an airtight container for up to 1 week or in the freezer for up to 3 months.

*T*his one-bowl recipe couldn't be easier or quicker to make. Perfect for when you have a huge craving for a fudgy, chewy cookie and no time . . . which is basically every moment of my life.

Chocolate Cherry Cookies

Makes 12 cookies

1½ cups icing sugar

½ cup dark cocoa

3 egg whites

1 egg

1 teaspoon pure vanilla

1 cup self-rising pastry flour

½ teaspoon salt

1 cup dried sour cherries

½ cup semisweet chocolate chips

Preheat the oven to 350°F. Line two cookie sheets with parchment paper and set aside.

In a large mixing bowl, whisk together the icing sugar, cocoa, egg whites, egg, and vanilla by hand. Add the flour and salt and whisk again until smooth. Stir in the dried cherries and chocolate chips.

Use an ice-cream scoop to drop 12 equally sized portions of dough onto the prepared cookie sheets, about 1½ inches apart.

Bake for 8 minutes, until the edges are set and the cookies are still slightly soft in the center. Remove from the oven and transfer to wire racks to cool.

Store covered or in an airtight container for up to 1 week or in the freezer for up to 3 months.

*L*ight as air, these cookies are like little pavlova hand pies. They're crispy at first, but after they sit for a bit with their chocolate filling, they tend to soften up, just like the rest of us.

Coffee Meringue Sandwiches with Hazelnut Dust

Makes 12 sandwich cookies

¾ cup The Best Chocolate Sauce (page 267), slightly chilled

3 egg whites

½ teaspoon cream of tartar

¾ cup granulated sugar

½ teaspoon pure vanilla

2 teaspoons instant espresso powder

3 tablespoons finely chopped hazelnuts

Prepare the chocolate sauce (you want it to be slightly chilled to start, so consider making it the day before) and refrigerate until ready to use.

Preheat the oven to 250°F.

Start with two cookie sheet–sized pieces of parchment paper, and use a 2½-inch circular cutter to trace the outline of 12 circles per sheet, about 1 inch apart, on the back of each. Turn the papers right side up and place each on its own cookie sheet. The pencil tracings will show through the paper and act as a template when you're piping the cookies.

In a stand mixer fitted with the whisk attachment, beat the egg whites on high until foamy. Add the cream of tartar and continue to beat until soft peaks form. Turn the mixer to medium speed and slowly add the sugar, a couple of tablespoons at a time. Once all the sugar has been added, return the mixer to high speed and beat until shiny, stiff peaks form. You can test this by turning off the mixer, sticking your spatula into the egg whites, and quickly pulling it out. When you hold the spatula upright, the meringue should hold a stiff peak.

Add the vanilla and instant espresso powder and mix again.

Fill a 14-inch piping bag fitted with a star tip with the meringue. Hold the bag upright and pipe the meringue in circles on the parchment paper, using the circles you drew as your guide and starting at the outer edge and working toward the center. Continue until both trays are complete.

Sprinkle one tray of the meringue cookies with the chopped hazelnuts. These will be the tops of your cookies.

Follow me

Bake for 90 minutes, until the meringues are crisp and light to the touch. Turn off the oven and allow the cookies to sit undisturbed for at least 2 hours or overnight. Remove the cookies and allow them to cool completely before filling.

Warm the chocolate sauce in the microwave for about 20 seconds, until it is just soft enough to stir and become spreadable. Don't overheat it or things will get saucy.

Turn the 12 cookies without hazelnuts bottom side up and use a small offset spatula to spread about 1 tablespoon of the chocolate sauce on each one. Top with the remaining cookies and very gently press them together. Meringue is fragile and will crush if you're too rough.

Store in an airtight container for up to 3 days.

1½ cups heavy cream

¼ cup icing sugar

1 teaspoon pure vanilla

*T*he name kind of lays it all out there for you, but being a stickler for the details, just bear with me.

Whipped Cream

Makes a big bowlful

In a stand mixer fitted with the whisk attachment, whip the cream, sugar, and vanilla on high speed until soft peaks form. Store, covered, in the refrigerator for up to 2 days.

- 1 cup water
- ½ cup granulated sugar
- 1 cup dark cocoa
- 1 cup semisweet chocolate chips

So easy, so fast, and so chocolatey. It keeps in the refrigerator for at least 2 weeks, so you've got little excuse not to always have some on hand. You can drizzle it on top of ice cream or puddle it beside a slice of cake; stir it into warm milk for a perfect hot chocolate or let it firm up in the refrigerator just enough to spread inside cookies.

The Best Chocolate Sauce

Makes about 2 cups

In a small saucepan over medium-high heat, whisk together the water, sugar, and cocoa until the sugar has dissolved and the mixture has reached a low boil. Remove from the heat, add the chocolate chips, and whisk until fully combined and melted. Voilà!

MENU PLANS

I have this philosophy when shopping for clothes: don't come home without a complete outfit. There's nothing more frustrating than a closet full of random tops when you're trying to get dressed in the morning. So even if I love, love, *love* that blouse, I don't leave the store without a skirt or pants that fit with it. That's the way I feel about these menu plans. Think of them as a few complete "outfits" to get you started, and then you can mix and match my recipes with your existing meals at home.

Thank You

The list of people who deserve my heartfelt thanks for their help and support in the creation of this book is so long it deserves its own volume. It became very clear to me when writing about my life and the meals I make and share with family, friends, and customers on a daily basis that without them, I wouldn't have much of a story to tell. But in an effort to save printing costs, please know that if I've fed you, I love you.

I never imagined I would get to make one cookbook in my lifetime, let alone three! Robert McCullough and Lindsay Paterson of Appetite, you have made it all possible. I am so grateful for your constant support, trust, and friendship.

Kelly Hill, your talent is endless. Thank you for doing such a beautiful job of interpreting me and my serious love for blue stripes.

Janis Nicolay, you are quite simply the best, both photographer and person! I am so damn lucky I get to work with you.

My agent, Janis Donnaud, if this journey were a road trip I'd pick you to be designated navigator every time.

Josh Glover and the rest of the wonderful publicity, marketing and sales team at Penguin Random House, thank you for your creativity and support with my work.

A Purposeful Rescue, thank you for saving Pickle and bringing her into our lives. I am in awe of the fine work that you do for all the senior doggies out there.

Katie Caroll, thank goodness for your fine proofreading skills to make up for my serious lack of them.

India, I truly wrote this book for you. Nothing makes me happier than envisioning you cooking for your own family one day from these very pages. I love you so, so much.

And to Paul . . . It's you, Charlie. It's always been you.

xo

Index

cashews
    Nut Bars, 257
Cauliflower, Roasted, Soup with
    Bacon, 107
celery
    Basic Chicken Stock, 99
    Beef Stew with Dumplings, 173–74
    Chicken Pie, 169–70
    Classic Egg Salad Sandwich, 82
    Curried Chicken Sandwich, 85
    Gram's Spaghetti Sauce, 186
    Lox and Bagel Soup, 116
    Mushroom Pancetta Soup, 115
    Noodle Chicken Soup, 108
    Roasted Cauliflower Soup with
        Bacon, 107
    Tuna and Potato Chip Sandwich,
        88
Cheddar
    Broccoli, Ham, and Cheddar
        Quiche, 154
    Cheddar Cheese Crackers, 69
    Damn Good Meatloaf, 181
    Egg McWhatchamacallit, 40
    Fluffy Flaky Biscuits, 66
    Mac and Quintuple Cheese, 157
    Potato, Bacon, and Cheddar
        Quiche, 154
    Tomato Casserole, 199
cheese. See specific types
Cheesy Corn Bread, 59
cherries, dried
    Butter's Granola, 20
    Chocolate Cherry Cookies, 262
chicken
    Basic Chicken Stock, 99
    Chicken Pie, 169–70
    Clubhouse Chopped Salad, 138
    Curried Chicken Sandwich, 85
    Fried Chicken 2.0 (sandwich), 94
    Fried Chicken for Impatient People
        Like Me, 162
    I'd Rather Eat a C.A.B. than an
        Uber (sandwich), 95
    Noodle Chicken Soup, 108
    One-Pot Chicken Parm, 171–72
    Roasted Chicken with Dijon Herb
        Butter, 164–65

chickpeas
    Green Bean, Snow Pea, and Red
        Pepper Salad, 141
    Italian Sausage Sauce Soup, 119
Chili, Turkey, 161
chilies. See jalapeño peppers; poblano
        peppers
chocolate
    Bajillionaire Bars, 258
    Best Chocolate Sauce, The, 267
    Chocolate Berry Shortcake, 242–43
    Chocolate Cherry Cookies, 262
Chorizo, Green Beans with Cherry
        Tomatoes, Goat Cheese, and, 202
Cinnamon Doughnut Muffins, 33
Classic Egg Salad Sandwich, 82
Clubhouse Chopped Salad, 138
coconut
    Butter's Granola, 20
    Go Bars, 39
Coffee Meringue Sandwiches with
        Hazelnut Dust, 265–66
Compote, Strawberry Rhubarb, 20
corn
    Corn, Tomato, Poblano Chili, and
        Monterey Jack Quiche, 154
    Corn Pudding, 208
    Turkey Chili, 161
Corn Bread, Cheesy, 59
Couscous and Zucchini Salad, 145
Crackers, Cheddar Cheese, 69
cranberries
    Curried Chicken Sandwich, 85
    Go Bars, 39
cream cheese
    Lox and Bagel Soup, 116
    Mac and Quintuple Cheese, 157
crème fraîche
    Corn Pudding, 208
    Crème Fraîche Bundt Cake, 248
    Little Gem with Breadcrumb Dust,
        133
    Parsnip, Pear, and Blue Cheese
        Soup, 112
Croissants, Apple Almond Double-
        Baked, 25
Croissants, Homemade, 61–65
Cupcakes, Pink Grapefruit, 237–38

Curried Carrot Soup, 111
Curried Chicken Sandwich, 85

D
Damn Good Meatloaf, 181
Dijon Herb Butter, 229
Don't Lift the Lid Potatoes, 210
Doughnut Muffins, Cinnamon, 33
Dumplings, Parsley, 174

E
eggplant
    One-Pot Chicken Parm, 171–72
    Roasted Veg, 205
eggs
    Best and Basic Quiche, The, 151
    Classic Egg Salad Sandwich, 82
    Clubhouse Chopped Salad, 138
    Egg McWhatchamacallit, 40
    Old-School Potato Salad, 125
English Muffins, Real, 53–54

F
Fennel and French Lentils Salad, 130
Feta and Watermelon Salad with
        Lime, 137
Figs, Whipped Ricotta with
        Hazelnuts, Honey, and, 78
Flaky Quiche Pastry, 152
Fluffy Flaky Biscuits, 66
Fluffy Mashed Potatoes with Boursin
        Cheese, 212
Focaccia with a Salty Top, 50–51
French Lentils and Fennel Salad, 130
Fried Chicken 2.0 (sandwich), 94
Fried Chicken for Impatient People
        Like Me, 162
Fried Mushrooms with Sour Cream,
        204

G
goat cheese
    Asparagus and Goat Cheese Quiche,
        154